# GORGIAS

# GORGIAS

**PLATO**

*Translated*
**Benjamin Jowett**

GenNext Publication

*Published by*

GenNext Publication
5, Ansari Road
New Delhi-110002

*Distribution Network*
gyanbooks.com
India, USA, Canada, UK, Australia, France



ISBN: 978-93-5663-358-2 (HB)

15 impression 2024

*Printed at:* Goyal Offset Printers, Delhi.

# INTRODUCTION

In several of the dialogues of Plato, doubts have arisen among his interpreters as to which of the various subjects discussed in them is the main thesis. The speakers have the freedom of conversation; no severe rules of art restrict them, and sometimes we are inclined to think, with one of the dramatis personae in the Theaetetus, that the digressions have the greater interest. Yet in the most irregular of the dialogues there is also a certain natural growth or unity; the beginning is not forgotten at the end, and numerous allusions and references are interspersed, which form the loose connecting links of the whole. We must not neglect this unity, but neither must we attempt to confine the Platonic dialogue on the Procrustean bed of a single idea. (Compare Introduction to the Phaedrus.)

Two tendencies seem to have beset the interpreters of Plato in this matter. First, they have endeavoured to hang the dialogues upon one another by the slightest threads; and have thus been led to opposite and contradictory assertions respecting their order and sequence. The mantle of Schleiermacher has descended upon his successors, who have applied his method with the most various results. The value and use of the method has been hardly, if at all, examined either by him or them. Secondly, they have extended almost indefinitely the scope of each separate dialogue; in this way they think that they have escaped all difficulties, not seeing that what they have gained in generality they have lost in truth and distinctness. Metaphysical conceptions easily pass into one another; and the simpler notions of antiquity, which we can only realize by an effort, imperceptibly blend with the more familiar theories of modern philosophers. An eye for proportion is needed (his own art of measuring) in the study of Plato, as well as of other great artists. We may hardly admit that the moral antithesis of good and pleasure, or the intellectual antithesis of knowledge and opinion, being and appearance, are never far off in a Platonic discussion. But because they are in the background, we should not bring them into the foreground, or expect to discern them equally in all the dialogues.

There may be some advantage in drawing out a little the main outlines of the building; but the use of this is limited, and may be easily exaggerated. We may give Plato too much system, and alter the natural form and connection of his thoughts. Under the idea that his dialogues are finished works of art, we may find a reason for everything, and lose the highest characteristic of art, which is simplicity. Most great works receive a new light from a new and original mind. But whether these new lights are true or only suggestive, will depend on their agreement with the spirit of Plato, and the amount of direct evidence which can be urged in support of them. When a theory is running away with us, criticism does a friendly office in counselling moderation, and recalling us to the indications of the text.

Like the Phaedrus, the Gorgias has puzzled students of Plato by the appearance of two or more subjects. Under the cover of rhetoric higher themes are introduced; the argument expands into a general view of the good and evil of man. After making an ineffectual attempt to obtain a sound definition of his art from Gorgias, Socrates assumes the existence of a universal art of flattery or simulation having several branches:–this is the genus of which rhetoric is only one, and not the highest species. To flattery is opposed the true and noble art of life which he who possesses seeks always to impart to others, and which at last triumphs, if not here, at any rate in another world. These two aspects of life and knowledge appear to be the two leading ideas of the dialogue. The true and the false in individuals and states, in the treatment of the soul as well as of the body, are conceived under the forms of true and false art. In the development of this opposition there arise various other questions, such as the two famous paradoxes of Socrates (paradoxes as they are to the world in general, ideals as they may be more worthily called): (1) that to do is worse than to suffer evil; and (2) that when a man has done evil he had better be punished than unpunished; to which may be added (3) a third Socratic paradox or ideal, that bad men do what they think best, but not what they desire, for the desire of all is towards the good. That pleasure is to be distinguished from good is proved by the simultaneousness of pleasure and pain, and by the possibility of the bad having in certain cases pleasures as great as those of the good, or even greater. Not merely rhetoricians, but poets, musicians, and other artists, the whole tribe of statesmen, past as well as present, are included in the class of flatterers. The true and false finally appear before the judgment-seat of the gods below.

The dialogue naturally falls into three divisions, to which the three characters of Gorgias, Polus, and Callicles respectively correspond; and the form and manner change with the stages of the argument. Socrates is deferential towards Gorgias, playful and yet cutting in dealing with the youthful Polus, ironical and sarcastic in his encounter with Callicles. In the first division the question is asked–What is rhetoric? To this there is no answer given, for Gorgias is soon made to contradict himself by Socrates, and the argument is transferred to the hands of his disciple Polus, who rushes to the defence of his master. The answer has at last to be given by Socrates himself, but before he can even explain his meaning to Polus, he must enlighten him upon the great subject of shams or flatteries. When Polus finds his favourite art reduced to the level of cookery, he replies that at any rate rhetoricians, like despots, have great power. Socrates denies that they have any real power, and hence arise the three paradoxes already mentioned. Although they are strange to him, Polus is at last convinced of their truth; at least, they seem to him to follow legitimately from the premises. Thus the second act of the dialogue closes. Then Callicles appears on the scene, at first maintaining that pleasure is good, and that might is right, and that law is nothing but the combination of the many weak against the few strong. When he is confuted he withdraws from the argument, and leaves Socrates to arrive at the conclusion by himself. The conclusion is that there are two kinds of statesmanship, a higher and a lower–that which makes the people better, and that which only flatters them, and he exhorts Callicles to choose the higher. The dialogue terminates with a mythus of a final judgment, in which there will be no more flattery or disguise, and no further use for the teaching of rhetoric.

The characters of the three interlocutors also correspond to the parts which are assigned to them. Gorgias is the great rhetorician, now advanced in years, who goes from city to city displaying his talents, and is celebrated throughout Greece. Like all the Sophists in the dialogues of Plato, he is vain and boastful, yet he has also a certain dignity, and is treated by Socrates with considerable respect. But he is no match for him in dialectics. Although he has been teaching rhetoric all his life, he is still incapable of defining his own art. When his ideas begin to clear up, he is unwilling to admit that rhetoric can be wholly separated from justice and injustice, and this lingering sentiment of morality, or regard for public opinion, enables Socrates to detect him in a contradiction. Like Protagoras, he is described as of a generous nature; he expresses his approbation of Socrates' manner of approaching a question; he is quite "one of Socrates' sort, ready to be refuted as well as to refute," and very eager that Callicles and Socrates should have the game out. He knows by experience that rhetoric exercises great influence over other men, but he is unable to explain the puzzle how rhetoric can teach everything and know nothing.

Polus is an impetuous youth, a runaway "colt," as Socrates describes him, who wanted originally to have taken the place of Gorgias under the pretext that the old man was tired, and now avails himself of the earliest opportunity to enter the lists. He is said to be the author of a work on rhetoric, and is again mentioned in the Phaedrus, as the inventor of balanced or double forms of speech (compare Gorg.; Symp.). At first he is violent and ill-mannered, and is angry at seeing his master overthrown. But in the judicious hands of Socrates he is soon restored to good-humour, and compelled to assent to the required conclusion. Like Gorgias, he is overthrown because he compromises; he is unwilling to say that to do is fairer or more honourable than to suffer injustice. Though he is fascinated by the power of rhetoric, and dazzled by the splendour of success, he is not insensible to higher arguments. Plato may have felt that there would be an incongruity in a youth maintaining the cause of injustice against the world. He has never heard the other side of the question, and he listens to the paradoxes, as they appear to him, of Socrates with evident astonishment. He can hardly understand the meaning of Archelaus being miserable, or of rhetoric being only useful in self-accusation. When the argument with him has fairly run out.

Callicles, in whose house they are assembled, is introduced on the stage: he is with difficulty convinced that Socrates is in earnest; for if these things are true, then, as he says with real emotion, the foundations of society are upside down. In him another type of character is represented; he is neither sophist nor philosopher, but man of the world, and an accomplished Athenian gentleman. He might be described in modern language as a cynic or materialist, a lover of power and also of pleasure, and unscrupulous in his means of attaining both. There is no desire on his part to offer any compromise in the interests of morality; nor is any concession made by him. Like Thrasymachus in the Republic, though he is not of the same weak and vulgar class, he consistently maintains that might is right. His great motive of action is political ambition; in this he is characteristically Greek. Like Anytus in the Meno, he is the enemy of the Sophists; but favours the new art of rhetoric, which he regards as an excellent weapon of attack and defence. He is a despiser of mankind as he is of philosophy, and sees in the laws of the state only a violation of the order of nature, which intended that the stronger should govern the weaker (compare Republic). Like other men of the world who are of a speculative turn of mind, he generalizes the bad side of human nature, and has easily brought down his principles to his practice. Philosophy and poetry alike supply him with distinctions suited to his view of human life. He has a good will to Socrates, whose talents he evidently admires, while he censures the puerile use which he makes of them. He expresses a keen intellectual interest in the argument. Like Anytus, again, he has a sympathy with other men of the world; the Athenian statesmen of a former generation, who showed no weakness and made no mistakes, such as Miltiades, Themistocles, Pericles, are his favourites. His ideal of human character is a man of great passions and great powers, which he has developed to the utmost, and which he uses in his own enjoyment and in the government of others. Had Critias been the name instead of Callicles, about whom we know nothing from other sources, the opinions of the man would have seemed to reflect the history of his life.

And now the combat deepens. In Callicles, far more than in any sophist or rhetorician, is concentrated the spirit of evil against which Socrates is contending, the spirit of the world, the spirit of the many contending against the one wise man, of which the Sophists, as he describes them in the Republic, are the imitators rather than the authors, being themselves carried away by the great tide of public opinion. Socrates approaches his antagonist warily from a distance, with a sort of irony which touches with a light hand both his personal vices (probably in allusion to some scandal of the day) and his servility to the populace. At the same time, he is in most profound earnest, as Chaerephon remarks. Callicles soon loses his temper, but the more he is irritated, the more provoking and matter of fact does Socrates become. A repartee of his which appears to have been really made to the "omniscient" Hippias, according to the testimony of

Xenophon (Mem.), is introduced. He is called by Callicles a popular declaimer, and certainly shows that he has the power, in the words of Gorgias, of being "as long as he pleases," or "as short as he pleases" (compare Protag.). Callicles exhibits great ability in defending himself and attacking Socrates, whom he accuses of trifling and word-splitting; he is scandalized that the legitimate consequences of his own argument should be stated in plain terms; after the manner of men of the world, he wishes to preserve the decencies of life. But he cannot consistently maintain the bad sense of words; and getting confused between the abstract notions of better, superior, stronger, he is easily turned round by Socrates, and only induced to continue the argument by the authority of Gorgias. Once, when Socrates is describing the manner in which the ambitious citizen has to identify himself with the people, he partially recognizes the truth of his words.

The Socrates of the Gorgias may be compared with the Socrates of the Protagoras and Meno. As in other dialogues, he is the enemy of the Sophists and rhetoricians; and also of the statesmen, whom he regards as another variety of the same species. His behaviour is governed by that of his opponents; the least forwardness or egotism on their part is met by a corresponding irony on the part of Socrates. He must speak, for philosophy will not allow him to be silent. He is indeed more ironical and provoking than in any other of Plato's writings: for he is "fooled to the top of his bent" by the worldliness of Callicles. But he is also more deeply in earnest. He rises higher than even in the Phaedo and Crito: at first enveloping his moral convictions in a cloud of dust and dialectics, he ends by losing his method, his life, himself, in them. As in the Protagoras and Phaedrus, throwing aside the veil of irony, he makes a speech, but, true to his character, not until his adversary has refused to answer any more questions. The presentiment of his own fate is hanging over him. He is aware that Socrates, the single real teacher of politics, as he ventures to call himself, cannot safely go to war with the whole world, and that in the courts of earth he will be condemned. But he will be justified in the world below. Then the position of Socrates and Callicles will be reversed; all those things "unfit for ears polite" which Callicles has prophesied as likely to happen to him in this life, the insulting language, the box on the ears, will recoil upon his assailant. (Compare Republic, and the similar reversal of the position of the lawyer and the philosopher in the Theaetetus).

There is an interesting allusion to his own behaviour at the trial of the generals after the battle of Arginusae, which he ironically attributes to his ignorance of the manner in which a vote of the assembly should be taken. This is said to have happened "last year" (B.C. 406), and therefore the assumed date of the dialogue has been fixed at 405 B.C., when Socrates would already have been an old man. The date is clearly marked, but is scarcely reconcilable with another indication of time, viz. the "recent" usurpation of Archelaus, which occurred in the year 413; and still less with the "recent" death of Pericles, who really died twenty-four years previously (429 B.C.) and is afterwards reckoned among the statesmen of a past age; or with the mention of Nicias, who died in 413, and is nevertheless spoken of as a living witness. But we shall hereafter have reason to observe, that although there is a general consistency of times and persons in the Dialogues of Plato, a precise dramatic date is an invention of his commentators (Preface to Republic).

The conclusion of the Dialogue is remarkable, (1) for the truly characteristic declaration of Socrates that he is ignorant of the true nature and bearing of these things, while he affirms at the same time that no one can maintain any other view without being ridiculous. The profession of ignorance reminds us of the earlier and more exclusively Socratic Dialogues. But neither in them, nor in the Apology, nor in the Memorabilia of Xenophon, does Socrates express any doubt of the fundamental truths of morality. He evidently regards this "among the multitude of questions" which agitate human life "as the principle which alone remains unshaken." He does not insist here, any more than in the Phaedo, on the literal truth of the myth, but only on the soundness of the doctrine which is contained in it, that doing wrong is worse than suffering, and that a man should be rather than seem; for the next best thing to a man's being just is that he should be corrected and become just; also that he should avoid all flattery, whether of himself or of others; and that rhetoric should be employed for the maintenance of the right only. The revelation of another life is a recapitulation of the argument in a figure.

(2) Socrates makes the singular remark, that he is himself the only true politician of his age. In other passages, especially in the Apology, he disclaims being a politician at all. There he is convinced that he or any other good man who attempted to resist the popular will would be put to death before he had done any good to himself or others. Here he anticipates such a fate for himself, from the fact that he is "the only man of the present day who performs his public duties at all." The two points of view are not really inconsistent, but the difference between them is worth noticing: Socrates is and is not a public man. Not in the ordinary sense, like Alcibiades or Pericles, but in a higher one; and this will sooner or later entail the same consequences on him. He cannot be a private man if he would; neither can he separate morals from politics. Nor is he unwilling to be a politician, although he foresees the dangers which await him; but he must first become a better and wiser man, for he as well as Callicles is in a state of perplexity and uncertainty. And yet there is an inconsistency: for should not Socrates too have taught the citizens better than to put him to death?

And now, as he himself says, we will "resume the argument from the beginning."

Socrates, who is attended by his inseparable disciple, Chaerephon, meets Callicles in the streets of Athens. He is informed that he has just missed an exhibition of Gorgias, which he regrets, because he was desirous, not of hearing Gorgias display his rhetoric, but of interrogating him concerning the nature of his art. Callicles proposes that they shall go with him to his own house, where Gorgias is staying. There they find the great rhetorician and his younger friend and disciple Polus.

SOCRATES: Put the question to him, Chaerephon.

CHAEREPHON: What question?

SOCRATES: Who is he?–such a question as would elicit from a man the answer, "I am a cobbler."

Polus suggests that Gorgias may be tired, and desires to answer for him. "Who is Gorgias?" asks Chaerephon, imitating the manner of his master Socrates. "One of the best of men, and a proficient in the best and noblest of experimental arts," etc., replies Polus, in rhetorical and balanced phrases. Socrates is dissatisfied at the length and unmeaningness of the answer; he tells the disconcerted volunteer that he has mistaken the quality for the nature of the art, and remarks to Gorgias, that Polus has learnt how to make a speech, but not how to answer a question. He wishes that Gorgias would answer him. Gorgias is willing enough, and replies to the question asked by Chaerephon,–that he is a rhetorician, and in Homeric language, "boasts himself to be a good one." At the request of Socrates he promises to be brief; for "he can be as long as he pleases, and as short as he pleases." Socrates would have him bestow his length on others, and proceeds to ask him a number of questions, which are answered by him to his own great satisfaction, and with a brevity which excites the admiration of Socrates. The result of the discussion may be summed up as follows:–

Rhetoric treats of discourse; but music and medicine, and other particular arts, are also concerned with discourse; in what way then does rhetoric differ from them? Gorgias draws a distinction between the arts which deal with words, and the arts which have to do with external actions. Socrates extends this distinction further, and divides all productive arts into two classes: (1) arts which may be carried on in silence; and (2) arts which have to do with words, or in which words are coextensive with action, such as arithmetic, geometry, rhetoric. But still Gorgias could hardly have meant to say that arithmetic was the same as rhetoric. Even in the arts which are concerned with words there are differences. What then distinguishes rhetoric from the other arts which have to do with words? "The words which rhetoric uses relate to the best and greatest of human things." But tell me, Gorgias, what are the best? "Health first, beauty next, wealth third," in the words of the old song, or how would you rank them? The arts will come to you in a body, each claiming precedence and saying that her own good is superior to that of the rest– How will you choose between them? "I should say, Socrates, that the art of persuasion, which gives freedom to all men, and to individuals power in the state, is the greatest good." But what is the exact nature of this persuasion?–is the persevering retort: You could not describe Zeuxis as a painter, or even as a painter of figures, if there were other painters of figures; neither can you define rhetoric simply as an art of persuasion, because there are other arts which persuade, such as arithmetic, which is an art of persuasion about odd and even numbers. Gorgias is made to see the necessity of a further limitation, and he now defines rhetoric as the art of persuading in the law courts, and in the assembly, about the just and unjust. But still there are two sorts of persuasion: one which gives knowledge, and another which gives belief without knowledge; and knowledge is always true, but belief may be either true or false,–there is therefore a further question: which of the two sorts of persuasion does rhetoric effect in courts of law and assemblies? Plainly that which gives belief and not that which gives knowledge; for no one can impart a real knowledge of such matters to a crowd of persons in a few minutes. And there is another point to be considered:–when the assembly meets to advise about walls or docks or military expeditions, the rhetorician is not taken into counsel, but the architect, or the general. How would Gorgias explain this phenomenon? All who intend to become disciples, of whom there are several in the company, and not Socrates only, are eagerly asking:–About what then will rhetoric teach us to persuade or advise the state?

Gorgias illustrates the nature of rhetoric by adducing the example of Themistocles, who persuaded the Athenians to build their docks and walls, and of Pericles, whom Socrates himself has heard speaking about the middle wall of the Piraeus. He adds that he has exercised a similar power over the patients of his brother Herodicus. He could be chosen a physician by the assembly if he pleased, for no physician could compete with a rhetorician in popularity and influence. He could persuade the multitude of anything by the power of his rhetoric; not that the rhetorician ought to abuse this power any more than a boxer should abuse the art of self-defence. Rhetoric is a good thing, but, like all good things, may be unlawfully used. Neither is the teacher of the art to be deemed unjust because his pupils are unjust and make a bad use of the lessons which they have learned from him.

Socrates would like to know before he replies, whether Gorgias will quarrel with him if he points out a slight inconsistency into which he has fallen, or whether he, like himself, is one who loves to be refuted. Gorgias declares that he is quite one of his sort, but fears that the argument may be tedious to the company. The company cheer, and Chaerephon and Callicles exhort them to proceed. Socrates gently points out the supposed inconsistency into which Gorgias appears to have fallen, and which he is inclined to think may arise out of a misapprehension of his own. The rhetorician has been declared by Gorgias to be more persuasive to the ignorant than the physician, or any other expert. And he is said to be ignorant, and this ignorance of his is regarded by Gorgias as a happy condition, for he has escaped the trouble of learning. But is he as ignorant of just and unjust as he is of medicine or building? Gorgias is compelled to admit that if he did not know them previously he must learn them from his teacher as a part of the art of rhetoric. But he who has learned carpentry is a carpenter, and he who has learned music is a musician, and he who has learned justice is just. The rhetorician then must be a just man, and rhetoric is a just thing. But Gorgias has already admitted the opposite of this, viz. that rhetoric may be abused, and that the rhetorician may act unjustly. How is the inconsistency to be explained?

The fallacy of this argument is twofold; for in the first place, a man may know justice and not be just–here is the old confusion of the arts and the virtues;–nor can any teacher be expected to counteract wholly the bent of natural character; and secondly, a man may have a degree of justice, but not sufficient to prevent him from ever doing wrong. Polus is naturally exasperated at the sophism, which he is unable to detect; of course, he says, the rhetorician, like every one else, will admit that he knows justice (how can he do otherwise when pressed by the interrogations of Socrates?), but he thinks that great want of manners is shown in bringing the argument to such a pass. Socrates ironically replies, that when old men trip, the young set them on their legs again; and he is quite willing to retract, if he can be shown to be in error, but upon one condition, which is that Polus studies brevity. Polus is in great indignation at not being allowed to use as many words as he pleases in the free state of Athens. Socrates retorts, that yet harder will be his own case, if he is compelled to stay and listen to them. After some altercation they agree (compare Protag.), that Polus shall ask and Socrates answer.

"What is the art of Rhetoric?" says Polus. Not an art at all, replies Socrates, but a thing which in your book you affirm to have created art. Polus asks, "What thing?" and Socrates answers, An experience or routine of making a sort of delight or gratification. "But is not rhetoric a fine thing?" I have not yet told you what rhetoric is. Will you ask me another question–What is cookery? "What is cookery?" An experience or routine of making a sort of delight or gratification. Then they are the same, or rather fall under the same class, and rhetoric has still to be distinguished from cookery. "What is rhetoric?" asks Polus once more. A part of a not very creditable whole, which may be termed flattery, is the reply. "But what part?" A shadow of a part of politics.

This, as might be expected, is wholly unintelligible, both to Gorgias and Polus; and, in order to explain his meaning to them, Socrates draws a distinction between shadows or appearances and realities; e.g. there is real health of body or soul, and the appearance of them; real arts and sciences, and the simulations of them. Now the soul and body have two arts waiting upon them, first the art of politics, which attends on the soul, having a legislative part and a judicial part; and another art attending on the body, which has no generic name, but may also be described as having two divisions, one of which is medicine and the other gymnastic. Corresponding with these four arts or sciences there are four shams or simulations of them, mere experiences, as they may be termed, because they give no reason of their own existence. The art of dressing up is the sham or simulation of gymnastic, the art of cookery, of medicine; rhetoric is the simulation of justice, and sophistic of legislation. They may be summed up in an arithmetical formula:–

Tiring: gymnastic:: cookery: medicine:: sophistic: legislation.

And,

Cookery: medicine:: rhetoric: the art of justice.

And this is the true scheme of them, but when measured only by the gratification which they procure, they become jumbled together and return to their aboriginal chaos. Socrates apologizes for the length of his speech, which was necessary to the explanation of the subject, and begs Polus not unnecessarily to retaliate on him.

"Do you mean to say that the rhetoricians are esteemed flatterers?" They are not esteemed at all. "Why, have they not great power, and can they not do whatever they desire?" They have no power, and they only do what they think best, and never what they desire; for they never attain the true object of desire, which is the good. "As if you, Socrates, would not envy the possessor of despotic power, who can imprison, exile, kill any one whom he pleases." But Socrates replies that he has no wish to put any one to death; he who kills another, even justly, is not to be envied, and he who kills him unjustly is to be pitied; it is better to suffer than to do injustice. He does not consider that going about with a dagger and putting men out of the way, or setting a house on fire, is real power. To this Polus assents, on the ground that such acts would be punished, but he is still of opinion that evil-doers, if they are unpunished, may be happy enough. He instances Archelaus, son of Perdiccas, the usurper of Macedonia. Does not Socrates think him happy?–Socrates would like to know more about him; he cannot pronounce even the great king to be happy, unless he knows his mental and moral condition. Polus explains that Archelaus was a slave, being the son of a woman who was the slave of Alcetas, brother of Perdiccas king of Macedon–and he, by every species of crime, first murdering his uncle and then his cousin and half-brother, obtained the kingdom. This was very wicked, and yet all the world, including Socrates, would like to have his place. Socrates dismisses the appeal to numbers; Polus, if he will, may summon all the rich men of Athens, Nicias and his brothers, Aristocrates, the house of Pericles, or any other great family–this is the kind of evidence which is adduced in courts of justice, where truth depends upon numbers. But Socrates employs proof of another sort; his appeal is to one witness only,–that is to say, the person with whom he is speaking; him he will convict out of his own mouth. And he is prepared to show, after his manner, that Archelaus cannot be a wicked man and yet happy.

The evil-doer is deemed happy if he escapes, and miserable if he suffers punishment; but Socrates thinks him less miserable if he suffers than if he escapes. Polus is of opinion that such a paradox as this hardly deserves refutation, and is at any rate sufficiently refuted by the fact. Socrates has only to compare the lot of the successful tyrant who is the envy of the world, and of the wretch who, having been detected in a criminal attempt against the state, is crucified or burnt to death. Socrates replies, that if they are both criminal they are both miserable, but that the unpunished is the more miserable of the two. At this Polus laughs outright, which leads Socrates to remark that laughter is a new species of refutation. Polus replies, that he is already refuted; for if he will take the votes of the company, he will find that no one agrees with him. To this Socrates rejoins, that he is not a public man, and (referring to his own conduct at the trial of the generals after the battle of Arginusae) is unable to take the suffrages of any company, as he had shown on a recent occasion; he can only deal with one witness at a time, and that is the person with whom he is arguing. But he is certain that in the opinion of any man to do is worse than to suffer evil.

Polus, though he will not admit this, is ready to acknowledge that to do evil is considered the more foul or dishonourable of the two. But what is fair and what is foul; whether the terms are applied to bodies, colours, figures, laws, habits, studies, must they not be defined with reference to pleasure and utility? Polus assents to this latter doctrine, and is easily persuaded that the fouler of two things must exceed either in pain or in hurt. But the doing cannot exceed the suffering of evil in pain, and therefore must exceed in hurt. Thus doing is proved by the testimony of Polus himself to be worse or more hurtful than suffering.

There remains the other question: Is a guilty man better off when he is punished or when he is unpunished? Socrates replies, that what is done justly is suffered justly: if the act is just, the effect is just; if to punish is just, to be punished is just, and therefore fair, and therefore beneficent; and the benefit is that the soul is improved. There are three evils from which a man may suffer, and which affect him in estate, body, and soul;–these are, poverty, disease, injustice; and the foulest of these is injustice, the evil of the soul, because that brings the greatest hurt. And there are three arts which heal these evils–trading, medicine, justice–and the fairest of these is justice. Happy is he who has never committed injustice, and happy in the second degree he who has been healed by punishment. And therefore the criminal should himself go to the judge as he would to the physician, and purge away his crime. Rhetoric will enable him to display his guilt in proper colours, and to sustain himself and others in enduring the necessary penalty. And similarly if a man has an enemy, he will desire not to punish him, but that he shall go unpunished and become worse and worse, taking care only that he does no injury to himself. These are at least conceivable uses of the art, and no others have been discovered by us.

Here Callicles, who has been listening in silent amazement, asks Chaerephon whether Socrates is in earnest, and on receiving the assurance that he is, proceeds to ask the same question of Socrates himself. For if such doctrines are true, life must have been turned upside down, and all of us are doing the opposite of what we ought to be doing.

Socrates replies in a style of playful irony, that before men can understand one another they must have some common feeling. And such a community of feeling exists between himself and Callicles, for both of them are lovers, and they have both a pair of loves; the beloved of Callicles are the Athenian Demos and Demos the son of Pyrilampes; the beloved of Socrates are Alcibiades and philosophy. The peculiarity of Callicles is that he can never contradict his loves; he changes as his Demos changes in all his opinions; he watches the countenance of both his loves, and repeats their sentiments, and if any one is surprised at his sayings and doings, the explanation of them is, that he is not a free agent, but must always be imitating his two loves. And this is the explanation of Socrates' peculiarities also. He is always repeating what his mistress, Philosophy, is saying to him, who unlike his other love, Alcibiades, is ever the same, ever true. Callicles must refute her, or he will never be at unity with himself; and discord in life is far worse than the discord of musical sounds.

Callicles answers, that Gorgias was overthrown because, as Polus said, in compliance with popular prejudice he had admitted that if his pupil did not know justice the rhetorician must teach him; and Polus has been similarly entangled, because his modesty led him to admit that to suffer is more honourable than to do injustice. By custom "yes," but not by nature, says Callicles. And Socrates is always playing between the two points of view, and putting one in the place of the other. In this very argument, what Polus only meant in a conventional sense has been affirmed by him to be a law of nature. For convention says that "injustice is dishonourable," but nature says that "might is right." And we are always taming down the nobler spirits among us to the conventional level. But sometimes a great man will rise up and reassert his original rights, trampling under foot all our formularies, and then the light of natural justice shines forth. Pindar says, "Law, the king of all, does violence with high hand;" as is indeed proved by the example of Heracles, who drove off the oxen of Geryon and never paid for them.

This is the truth, Socrates, as you will be convinced, if you leave philosophy and pass on to the real business of life. A little philosophy is an excellent thing; too much is the ruin of a man. He who has not "passed his metaphysics" before he has grown up to manhood will never know the world. Philosophers are ridiculous when they take to politics, and I dare say that politicians are equally ridiculous when they take to philosophy: "Every man," as Euripides says, "is fondest of that in which he is best." Philosophy is graceful in youth, like the lisp of infancy, and should be cultivated as a part of education; but when a grown-up man lisps or studies philosophy, I should like to beat him. None of those over-refined natures ever come to any good; they avoid the busy haunts of men, and skulk in corners, whispering to a few admiring youths, and never giving utterance to any noble sentiments.

For you, Socrates, I have a regard, and therefore I say to you, as Zethus says to Amphion in the play, that you have "a noble soul disguised in a puerile exterior." And I would have you consider the danger which you and other philosophers incur. For you would not know how to defend yourself if any one accused you in a law-court,–there you would stand, with gaping mouth and dizzy brain, and might be murdered, robbed, boxed on the ears with impunity. Take my advice, then, and get a little common sense; leave to others these frivolities; walk in the ways of the wealthy and be wise.

Socrates professes to have found in Callicles the philosopher's touchstone; and he is certain that any opinion in which they both agree must be the very truth. Callicles has all the three qualities which are needed in a critic–knowledge, good-will, frankness; Gorgias and Polus, although learned men, were too modest, and their modesty made them contradict themselves. But Callicles is well-educated; and he is not too modest to speak out (of this he has already given proof), and his good-will is shown both by his own profession and by his giving the same caution against philosophy to Socrates, which Socrates remembers hearing him give long ago to his own clique of friends. He will pledge himself to retract any error into which he may have fallen, and which Callicles may point out. But he would like to know first of all what he and Pindar mean by natural justice. Do they suppose that the rule of justice is the rule of the stronger or of the better? "There is no difference." Then are not the many superior to the one, and the opinions of the many better? And their opinion is that justice is equality, and that to do is more dishonourable than to suffer wrong. And as they are the superior or stronger, this opinion of theirs must be in accordance with natural as well as conventional justice. "Why will you continue splitting words? Have I not told you that the superior is the better?" But what do you mean by the better? Tell me that, and please to be a little milder in your language, if you do not wish to drive me away. "I mean the worthier, the wiser." You mean to say that one man of sense ought to rule over ten thousand fools? "Yes, that is my meaning." Ought the physician then to have a larger share of meats and drinks? or the weaver to have more coats, or the cobbler larger shoes, or the farmer more seed? "You are always saying the same things, Socrates." Yes, and on the same subjects too; but you are never saying the same things. For, first, you defined the superior to be the stronger, and then the wiser, and now something else;–what DO you mean? "I mean men of political ability, who ought to govern and to have more than the governed." Than themselves? "What do you mean?" I mean to say that every man is his own governor. "I see that you mean those dolts, the temperate. But my doctrine is, that a man should let his desires grow, and take the means of satisfying them. To the many this is impossible, and therefore they combine to prevent him. But if he is a king, and has power, how base would he be in submitting to them! To invite the common herd to be lord over him, when he might have the enjoyment of all things! For the truth is, Socrates, that luxury and self-indulgence are virtue and happiness; all the rest is mere talk."

Socrates compliments Callicles on his frankness in saying what other men only think. According to his view, those who want nothing are not happy. "Why," says Callicles, "if they were, stones and the dead would be happy." Socrates in reply is led into a half-serious, half-comic vein of reflection. "Who knows," as Euripides says, "whether life may not be death, and death life?" Nay, there are philosophers who maintain that even in life we are dead, and that the body (soma) is the tomb (sema) of the soul. And some ingenious Sicilian has made an allegory, in which he represents fools as the uninitiated, who are supposed to be carrying water to a vessel, which is full of holes, in a similarly holey sieve, and this sieve is their own soul. The idea is fanciful, but nevertheless is a figure of a truth which I want to make you acknowledge, viz. that the life of contentment is better than the life of indulgence. Are you disposed to admit that? "Far otherwise." Then hear another parable. The life of self-contentment and self-indulgence may be represented respectively by two men, who are filling jars with streams of wine, honey, milk,–the jars of the one are sound, and the jars of the other leaky;

the first fills his jars, and has no more trouble with them; the second is always filling them, and would suffer extreme misery if he desisted. Are you of the same opinion still? "Yes, Socrates, and the figure expresses what I mean. For true pleasure is a perpetual stream, flowing in and flowing out. To be hungry and always eating, to be thirsty and always drinking, and to have all the other desires and to satisfy them, that, as I admit, is my idea of happiness." And to be itching and always scratching? "I do not deny that there may be happiness even in that." And to indulge unnatural desires, if they are abundantly satisfied? Callicles is indignant at the introduction of such topics. But he is reminded by Socrates that they are introduced, not by him, but by the maintainer of the identity of pleasure and good. Will Callicles still maintain this? "Yes, for the sake of consistency, he will." The answer does not satisfy Socrates, who fears that he is losing his touchstone. A profession of seriousness on the part of Callicles reassures him, and they proceed with the argument. Pleasure and good are the same, but knowledge and courage are not the same either with pleasure or good, or with one another. Socrates disproves the first of these statements by showing that two opposites cannot coexist, but must alternate with one another–to be well and ill together is impossible. But pleasure and pain are simultaneous, and the cessation of them is simultaneous; e.g. in the case of drinking and thirsting, whereas good and evil are not simultaneous, and do not cease simultaneously, and therefore pleasure cannot be the same as good.

Callicles has already lost his temper, and can only be persuaded to go on by the interposition of Gorgias. Socrates, having already guarded against objections by distinguishing courage and knowledge from pleasure and good, proceeds:– The good are good by the presence of good, and the bad are bad by the presence of evil. And the brave and wise are good, and the cowardly and foolish are bad. And he who feels pleasure is good, and he who feels pain is bad, and both feel pleasure and pain in nearly the same degree, and sometimes the bad man or coward in a greater degree. Therefore the bad man or coward is as good as the brave or may be even better.

Callicles endeavours now to avert the inevitable absurdity by affirming that he and all mankind admitted some pleasures to be good and others bad. The good are the beneficial, and the bad are the hurtful, and we should choose the one and avoid the other. But this, as Socrates observes, is a return to the old doctrine of himself and Polus, that all things should be done for the sake of the good.

Callicles assents to this, and Socrates, finding that they are agreed in distinguishing pleasure from good, returns to his old division of empirical habits, or shams, or flatteries, which study pleasure only, and the arts which are concerned with the higher interests of soul and body. Does Callicles agree to this division? Callicles will agree to anything, in order that he may get through the argument. Which of the arts then are flatteries? Flute-playing, harp-playing, choral exhibitions, the dithyrambics of Cinesias are all equally condemned on the ground that they give pleasure only; and Meles the harp-player, who was the father of Cinesias, failed even in that. The stately muse of Tragedy is bent upon pleasure, and not upon improvement. Poetry in general is only a rhetorical address to a mixed audience of men, women, and children. And the orators are very far from speaking with a view to what is best; their way is to humour the assembly as if they were children.

Callicles replies, that this is only true of some of them; others have a real regard for their fellow-citizens. Granted; then there are two species of oratory; the one a flattery, another which has a real regard for the citizens. But where are the orators among whom you find the latter? Callicles admits that there are none remaining, but there were such in the days when Themistocles, Cimon, Miltiades, and the great Pericles were still alive. Socrates replies that none of these were true artists, setting before themselves the duty of bringing order out of disorder. The good man and true orator has a settled design, running through his life, to which he conforms all his words and actions; he desires to implant justice and eradicate injustice, to implant all virtue and eradicate all vice in the minds of his citizens. He is the physician who will not allow the sick man to indulge his appetites with a variety of meats and drinks, but insists on his exercising self-restraint. And this is good for the soul, and better than the unrestrained indulgence which Callicles was recently approving.

Here Callicles, who had been with difficulty brought to this point, turns restive, and suggests that Socrates shall answer his own questions. "Then," says Socrates, "one man must do for two;" and though he had hoped to have given Callicles an "Amphion" in return for his "Zethus," he is willing to proceed; at the same time, he hopes that Callicles will correct him, if he falls into error. He recapitulates the advantages which he has already won:–

The pleasant is not the same as the good–Callicles and I are agreed about that,–but pleasure is to be pursued for the sake of the good, and the good is that of which the presence makes us good; we and all things good have acquired some virtue or other. And virtue, whether of body or soul, of things or persons, is not attained by accident, but is due to order and harmonious arrangement. And the soul which has order is better than the soul which is without order, and is therefore temperate and is therefore good, and the intemperate is bad. And he who is temperate is also just and brave and pious, and has attained the perfection of goodness and therefore of happiness, and the intemperate whom you approve is the opposite of all this and is wretched. He therefore who would be happy must pursue temperance and avoid intemperance, and if possible escape the necessity of punishment, but if he have done wrong he must endure punishment. In this way states and individuals should seek to attain harmony, which, as the wise tell us, is the bond of heaven and earth, of gods and men. Callicles has never discovered the power of geometrical proportion in both worlds; he would have men aim at disproportion and excess. But if he be wrong in this, and if self-control is the true secret of happiness, then the paradox is true that the only use of rhetoric is in self-accusation, and Polus was right in saying that to do wrong is worse than to suffer wrong, and Gorgias was right in saying that the rhetorician must be a just man. And you were wrong in taunting me with my defenceless condition, and in saying that I might be accused or put to death or boxed on the ears with impunity. For I may repeat once more, that to strike is worse than to be stricken–to do than to suffer. What I said then is now made fast in adamantine bonds. I myself know not the true nature of these things, but I know that no one can deny my words and not be ridiculous. To do wrong is the greatest of evils, and to suffer wrong is the next greatest evil. He who would avoid the last must be a ruler, or the friend of a ruler; and to be the friend he must be the equal of the ruler, and must also resemble him. Under his protection he will suffer no evil, but will he also do no evil? Nay, will he not rather do all the evil which he can and escape? And in this way the greatest of all evils will befall him. "But this imitator of the tyrant," rejoins Callicles, "will kill any one who does not similarly imitate him." Socrates replies that he is not deaf, and that he has heard that repeated many times, and can only reply, that a bad man will kill a good one. "Yes, and that is the provoking thing." Not provoking to a man of sense who is not studying the arts which will preserve him from danger; and this, as you say, is the use of rhetoric in courts of justice. But how many other arts are there which also save men from death, and are yet quite humble in their pretensions–such as the art of swimming, or the art of the pilot? Does not the pilot do men at least as much service as the rhetorician, and yet for the voyage from Aegina to Athens he does not charge more than two obols, and when he disembarks is quite unassuming in his demeanour? The reason is that he is not certain whether he has done his passengers any good in saving them from death, if one of them is diseased in body, and still more if he is diseased in mind–who can say? The engineer too will often save whole cities, and yet you despise him, and would not allow your son to marry his daughter, or his son to marry yours. But what reason is there in this? For if virtue only means the saving of life, whether your own or another's, you have no right to despise him or any practiser of saving arts. But is not virtue something different from saving and being saved? I would have you rather consider whether you ought not to disregard length of life, and think only how you can live best, leaving all besides to the will of Heaven. For you must not expect to have influence either with the Athenian Demos or with Demos the son of Pyrilampes, unless you become like them. What do you say to this?

"There is some truth in what you are saying, but I do not entirely believe you."

That is because you are in love with Demos. But let us have a little more conversation. You remember the two processes–one which was directed to pleasure, the other which was directed to making men as good as possible. And those who have the care of the city should make the citizens as good as possible. But who would undertake a public building, if he had never had a teacher of the art of building, and had never constructed a building before? or who would undertake the duty of state-physician, if he had never cured either himself or any one else? Should we not examine him before we entrusted him with the office? And as Callicles is about to enter public life, should we not examine him? Whom has he made better? For we have already admitted that this is the statesman's proper business. And we must ask the same question about Pericles, and Cimon, and Miltiades, and Themistocles. Whom did they make better? Nay, did not Pericles make the citizens worse? For he gave them pay, and at first he was very popular with them, but at last they condemned him to death. Yet surely he would be a bad tamer of animals who, having received them gentle, taught them to kick and butt, and man is an animal; and Pericles who had the charge of man only made him wilder, and more savage and unjust, and therefore he could not have been a good statesman. The same tale might be repeated about Cimon, Themistocles, Miltiades. But the charioteer who keeps his seat at first is not thrown out when he gains greater experience and skill. The inference is, that the statesman of a past age were no better than those of our own. They may have been cleverer constructors of docks and harbours, but they did not improve the character of the citizens. I have told you again and again (and I purposely use the same images) that the soul, like the body, may be treated in two ways–there is the meaner and the higher art. You seemed to understand what I said at the time, but when I ask you who were the really good statesmen, you answer–as if I asked you who were the good trainers, and you answered, Thearion, the baker, Mithoecus, the author of the Sicilian cookery-book, Sarambus, the vintner. And you would be affronted if I told you that these are a parcel of cooks who make men fat only to make them thin. And those whom they have fattened applaud them, instead of finding fault with them, and lay the blame of their subsequent disorders on their physicians. In this respect, Callicles, you are like them; you applaud the statesmen of old, who pandered to the vices of the citizens, and filled the city with docks and harbours, but neglected virtue and justice. And when the fit of illness comes, the citizens who in like manner applauded Themistocles, Pericles, and others, will lay hold of you and my friend Alcibiades, and you will suffer for the misdeeds of your predecessors. The old story is always being repeated–"after all his services, the ungrateful city banished him, or condemned him to death." As if the statesman should not have taught the city better! He surely cannot blame the state for having unjustly used him, any more than the sophist or teacher can find fault with his pupils if they cheat him. And the sophist and orator are in the same case; although you admire rhetoric and despise sophistic, whereas sophistic is really the higher of the two. The teacher of the arts takes money, but the teacher of virtue or politics takes no money, because this is the only kind of service which makes the disciple desirous of requiting his teacher.

Socrates concludes by finally asking, to which of the two modes of serving the state Callicles invites him:–"to the inferior and ministerial one," is the ingenuous reply. That is the only way of avoiding death, replies Socrates; and he has heard often enough, and would rather not hear again, that the bad man will kill the good. But he thinks that such a fate is very likely reserved for him, because he remarks that he is the only person who teaches the true art of politics. And very probably, as in the case which he described to Polus, he may be the physician who is tried by a jury of children. He cannot say that he has procured the citizens any pleasure, and if any one charges him with perplexing them, or with reviling their elders, he will not be able to make them understand that he has only been actuated by a desire for their good. And therefore there is no saying what his fate may be. "And do you think that a man who is unable to help himself is in a good condition?" Yes, Callicles, if he have the true self-help, which is never to have said or done any wrong to himself or others. If I had not this kind of self-help, I should be ashamed; but if I die for want of your flattering rhetoric, I shall die in peace. For death is no evil, but to go to the world below laden with offences is the worst of evils. In proof of which I will tell you a tale:–

Under the rule of Cronos, men were judged on the day of their death, and when judgment had been given upon them they departed–the good to the islands of the blest, the bad to the house of vengeance. But as they were still living, and had their clothes on at the time when they were being judged, there was favouritism, and Zeus, when he came to the throne, was obliged to alter the mode of procedure, and try them after death, having first sent down Prometheus to take away from them the foreknowledge of death. Minos, Rhadamanthus, and Aeacus were appointed to be the judges; Rhadamanthus for Asia, Aeacus for Europe, and Minos was to hold the court of appeal. Now death is the separation of soul and body, but after death soul and body alike retain their characteristics; the fat man, the dandy, the branded slave, are all distinguishable. Some prince or potentate, perhaps even the great king himself, appears before Rhadamanthus, and he instantly detects him, though he knows not who he is; he sees the scars of perjury and iniquity, and sends him away to the house of torment.

For there are two classes of souls who undergo punishment–the curable and the incurable. The curable are those who are benefited by their punishment; the incurable are such as Archelaus, who benefit others by becoming a warning to them. The latter class are generally kings and potentates; meaner persons, happily for themselves, have not the same power of doing injustice. Sisyphus and Tityus, not Thersites, are supposed by Homer to be undergoing everlasting punishment. Not that there is anything to prevent a great man from being a good one, as is shown by the famous example of Aristeides, the son of Lysimachus. But to Rhadamanthus the souls are only known as good or bad; they are stripped of their dignities and preferments; he despatches the bad to Tartarus, labelled either as curable or incurable, and looks with love and admiration on the soul of some just one, whom he sends to the islands of the blest. Similar is the practice of Aeacus; and Minos overlooks them, holding a golden sceptre, as Odysseus in Homer saw him

*"Wielding a sceptre of gold, and giving laws to the dead."*

My wish for myself and my fellow-men is, that we may present our souls undefiled to the judge in that day; my desire in life is to be able to meet death. And I exhort you, and retort upon you the reproach which you cast upon me,–that you will stand before the judge, gaping, and with dizzy brain, and any one may box you on the ear, and do you all manner of evil.

Perhaps you think that this is an old wives' fable. But you, who are the three wisest men in Hellas, have nothing better to say, and no one will ever show that to do is better than to suffer evil. A man should study to be, and not merely to seem. If he is bad, he should become good, and avoid all flattery, whether of the many or of the few.

Follow me, then; and if you are looked down upon, that will do you no harm. And when we have practised virtue, we will betake ourselves to politics, but not until we are delivered from the shameful state of ignorance and uncertainty in which we are at present. Let us follow in the way of virtue and justice, and not in the way to which you, Callicles, invite us; for that way is nothing worth.

We will now consider in order some of the principal points of the dialogue. Having regard (1) to the age of Plato and the ironical character of his writings, we may compare him with himself, and with other great teachers, and we may note in passing the objections of his critics. And then (2) casting one eye upon him, we may cast another upon ourselves, and endeavour to draw out the great lessons which he teaches for all time, stripped of the accidental form in which they are enveloped.

(1) In the Gorgias, as in nearly all the other dialogues of Plato, we are made aware that formal logic has as yet no existence. The old difficulty of framing a definition recurs. The illusive analogy of the arts and the virtues also continues. The ambiguity of several words, such as nature, custom, the honourable, the good, is not cleared up. The Sophists are still floundering about the distinction of the real and seeming. Figures of speech are made the basis of arguments. The possibility of conceiving a universal art or science, which admits of application to a particular subject-matter, is a difficulty which remains unsolved, and has not altogether ceased to haunt the world at the present day (compare Charmides). The defect of clearness is also apparent in Socrates himself, unless we suppose him to be practising on the simplicity of his opponent, or rather perhaps trying an experiment in dialectics. Nothing can be more fallacious than the contradiction which he pretends to have discovered in the answers of Gorgias (see above). The advantages which he gains over Polus are also due to a false antithesis of pleasure

and good, and to an erroneous assertion that an agent and a patient may be described by similar predicates;–a mistake which Aristotle partly shares and partly corrects in the Nicomachean Ethics. Traces of a "robust sophistry" are likewise discernible in his argument with Callicles.

(2) Although Socrates professes to be convinced by reason only, yet the argument is often a sort of dialectical fiction, by which he conducts himself and others to his own ideal of life and action. And we may sometimes wish that we could have suggested answers to his antagonists, or pointed out to them the rocks which lay concealed under the ambiguous terms good, pleasure, and the like. But it would be as useless to examine his arguments by the requirements of modern logic, as to criticise this ideal from a merely utilitarian point of view. If we say that the ideal is generally regarded as unattainable, and that mankind will by no means agree in thinking that the criminal is happier when punished than when unpunished, any more than they would agree to the stoical paradox that a man may be happy on the rack, Plato has already admitted that the world is against him. Neither does he mean to say that Archelaus is tormented by the stings of conscience; or that the sensations of the impaled criminal are more agreeable than those of the tyrant drowned in luxurious enjoyment. Neither is he speaking, as in the Protagoras, of virtue as a calculation of pleasure, an opinion which he afterwards repudiates in the Phaedo. What then is his meaning? His meaning we shall be able to illustrate best by parallel notions, which, whether justifiable by logic or not, have always existed among mankind. We must remind the reader that Socrates himself implies that he will be understood or appreciated by very few.

He is speaking not of the consciousness of happiness, but of the idea of happiness. When a martyr dies in a good cause, when a soldier falls in battle, we do not suppose that death or wounds are without pain, or that their physical suffering is always compensated by a mental satisfaction. Still we regard them as happy, and we would a thousand times rather have their death than a shameful life. Nor is this only because we believe that they will obtain an immortality of fame, or that they will have crowns of glory in another world, when their enemies and persecutors will be proportionably tormented. Men are found in a few instances to do what is right, without reference to public opinion or to consequences. And we regard them as happy on this ground only, much as Socrates' friends in the opening of the Phaedo are described as regarding him; or as was said of another, "they looked upon his face as upon the face of an angel." We are not concerned to justify this idealism by the standard of utility or public opinion, but merely to point out the existence of such a sentiment in the better part of human nature.

The idealism of Plato is founded upon this sentiment. He would maintain that in some sense or other truth and right are alone to be sought, and that all other goods are only desirable as means towards these. He is thought to have erred in "considering the agent only, and making no reference to the happiness of others, as affected by him." But the happiness of others or of mankind, if regarded as an end, is really quite as ideal and almost as paradoxical to the common understanding as Plato's conception of happiness. For the greatest happiness of the greatest number may mean also the greatest pain of the individual which will procure the greatest pleasure of the greatest number. Ideas of utility, like those of duty and right, may be pushed to unpleasant consequences. Nor can Plato in the Gorgias be deemed purely self-regarding, considering that Socrates expressly mentions the duty of imparting the truth when discovered to others. Nor must we forget that the side of ethics which regards others is by the ancients merged in politics. Both in Plato and Aristotle, as well as in the Stoics, the social principle, though taking another form, is really far more prominent than in most modern treatises on ethics.

The idealizing of suffering is one of the conceptions which have exercised the greatest influence on mankind. Into the theological import of this, or into the consideration of the errors to which the idea may have given rise, we need not now enter. All will agree that the ideal of the Divine Sufferer, whose words the world would not receive, the man of sorrows of whom the Hebrew prophets spoke, has sunk deep into the heart of the human race. It is a similar picture of suffering goodness which Plato desires to pourtray, not without an allusion to the fate of his master Socrates. He is convinced that, somehow or other, such an one must be happy in life or after death. In the Republic, he endeavours to show that his happiness would be assured here in a well-ordered state. But in the actual condition of human things the wise and good are weak and miserable; such an one is like a man fallen among wild beasts, exposed to every sort of wrong and obloquy.

Plato, like other philosophers, is thus led on to the conclusion, that if "the ways of God" to man are to be "justified," the hopes of another life must be included. If the question could have been put to him, whether a man dying in torments was happy still, even if, as he suggests in the Apology, "death be only a long sleep," we can hardly tell what would have been his answer. There have been a few, who, quite independently of rewards and punishments or of posthumous reputation, or any other influence of public opinion, have been willing to sacrifice their lives for the good of others. It is difficult to say how far in such cases an unconscious hope of a future life, or a general faith in the victory of good in the world, may have supported the sufferers. But this extreme idealism is not in accordance with the spirit of Plato. He supposes a day of retribution, in which the good are to be rewarded and the wicked punished. Though, as he says in the Phaedo, no man of sense will maintain that the details of the stories about another world are true, he will insist that something of the kind is true, and will frame his life with a view to this unknown future. Even in the Republic he introduces a future life as an afterthought, when the superior happiness of the just has been established on what is thought to be an immutable foundation. At the same time he makes a point of determining his main thesis independently of remoter consequences.

(3) Plato's theory of punishment is partly vindictive, partly corrective. In the Gorgias, as well as in the Phaedo and Republic, a few great criminals, chiefly tyrants, are reserved as examples. But most men have never had the opportunity of attaining this pre-eminence of evil. They are not incurable, and their punishment is intended for their improvement. They are to suffer because they have sinned; like sick men, they must go to the physician and be healed. On this representation of Plato's the criticism has been made, that the analogy of disease and injustice is partial only, and that suffering, instead of improving men, may have just the opposite effect.

Like the general analogy of the arts and the virtues, the analogy of disease and injustice, or of medicine and justice, is certainly imperfect. But ideas must be given through something; the nature of the mind which is unseen can only be represented under figures derived from visible objects. If these figures are suggestive of some new aspect under which the mind may be considered, we cannot find fault with them for not exactly coinciding with the ideas represented. They partake of the imperfect nature of language, and must not be construed in too strict a manner. That Plato sometimes reasons from them as if they were not figures but realities, is due to the defective logical analysis of his age.

Nor does he distinguish between the suffering which improves and the suffering which only punishes and deters. He applies to the sphere of ethics a conception of punishment which is really derived from criminal law. He does not see that such punishment is only negative, and supplies no principle of moral growth or development. He is not far off the higher notion of an education of man to be begun in this world, and to be continued in other stages of existence, which is further developed in the Republic. And Christian thinkers, who have ventured out of the beaten track in their meditations on the "last things," have found a ray of light in his writings.

But he has not explained how or in what way punishment is to contribute to the improvement of mankind. He has not followed out the principle which he affirms in the Republic, that "God is the author of evil only with a view to good," and that "they were the better for being punished." Still his doctrine of a future state of rewards and punishments may be compared favourably with that perversion of Christian doctrine which makes the everlasting punishment of human beings depend on a brief moment of time, or even on the accident of an accident. And he has escaped the difficulty which has often beset divines, respecting the future destiny of the meaner sort of men (Thersites and the like), who are neither very good nor very bad, by not counting them worthy of eternal damnation.

We do Plato violence in pressing his figures of speech or chains of argument; and not less so in asking questions which were beyond the horizon of his vision, or did not come within the scope of his design. The main purpose of the Gorgias is not to answer questions about a future world, but to place in antagonism the true and false life, and to contrast the judgments and opinions of men with judgment according to the truth. Plato may be accused of representing a superhuman or transcendental virtue in the description of the just man in the Gorgias, or in the companion portrait of the philosopher in the Theaetetus; and at the same time may be thought to be condemning a state of the world which always has existed and always will exist among men. But such ideals act powerfully on the imagination of mankind. And such condemnations are not mere paradoxes of philosophers, but the natural rebellion of the higher sense of right in man against the ordinary conditions of human life. The greatest statesmen have fallen very far short of the political ideal, and are therefore justly involved in the general condemnation.

Subordinate to the main purpose of the dialogue are some other questions, which may be briefly considered:–

(a) The antithesis of good and pleasure, which as in other dialogues is supposed to consist in the permanent nature of the one compared with the transient and relative nature of the other. Good and pleasure, knowledge and sense, truth and opinion, essence and generation, virtue and pleasure, the real and the apparent, the infinite and finite, harmony or beauty and discord, dialectic and rhetoric or poetry, are so many pairs of opposites, which in Plato easily pass into one another, and are seldom kept perfectly distinct. And we must not forget that Plato's conception of pleasure is the Heracleitean flux transferred to the sphere of human conduct. There is some degree of unfairness in opposing the principle of good, which is objective, to the principle of pleasure, which is subjective. For the assertion of the permanence of good is only based on the assumption of its objective character. Had Plato fixed his mind, not on the ideal nature of good, but on the subjective consciousness of happiness, that would have been found to be as transient and precarious as pleasure.

(b) The arts or sciences, when pursued without any view to truth, or the improvement of human life, are called flatteries. They are all alike dependent upon the opinion of mankind, from which they are derived. To Plato the whole world appears to be sunk in error, based on self-interest. To this is opposed the one wise man hardly professing to have found truth, yet strong in the conviction that a virtuous life is the only good, whether regarded with reference to this world or to another. Statesmen, Sophists, rhetoricians, poets, are alike brought up for judgment. They are the parodies of wise men, and their arts are the parodies of true arts and sciences. All that they call science is merely the result of that study of the tempers of the Great Beast, which he describes in the Republic.

(c) Various other points of contact naturally suggest themselves between the Gorgias and other dialogues, especially the Republic, the Philebus, and the Protagoras. There are closer resemblances both of spirit and language in the Republic than in any other dialogue, the verbal similarity tending to show that they were written at the same period of Plato's life. For the Republic supplies that education and training of which the Gorgias suggests the necessity. The theory of the many weak combining against the few strong in the formation of society (which is indeed a partial truth), is similar in both of them, and is expressed in nearly the same language. The sufferings and fate of the just man, the powerlessness of evil, and the reversal of the situation in another life, are also points of similarity. The poets, like the rhetoricians, are condemned because they aim at pleasure only, as in the Republic they are expelled by the State, because they are imitators, and minister to the weaker side of human nature. That poetry is akin to rhetoric may be compared with the analogous notion, which occurs in the Protagoras, that the ancient poets were the Sophists of their day. In some other respects the Protagoras rather offers a contrast than a parallel. The character of Protagoras may be compared with that of Gorgias, but the conception of happiness is different in the two dialogues; being described in the former, according to the old Socratic notion, as deferred or accumulated pleasure, while in the Gorgias, and in the Phaedo, pleasure and good are distinctly opposed.

This opposition is carried out from a speculative point of view in the Philebus. There neither pleasure nor wisdom are allowed to be the chief good, but pleasure and good are not so completely opposed as in the Gorgias. For innocent pleasures, and such as have no antecedent pains, are allowed to rank in the class of goods. The allusion to Gorgias' definition of rhetoric (Philebus; compare Gorg.), as the art of persuasion, of all arts the best, for to it all things submit, not by compulsion, but of their own free will–marks a close and perhaps designed connection between the two dialogues. In both the ideas of measure, order, harmony, are the connecting links between the beautiful and the good.

In general spirit and character, that is, in irony and antagonism to public opinion, the Gorgias most nearly resembles the Apology, Crito, and portions of the Republic, and like the Philebus, though from another point of view, may be thought to stand in the same relation to Plato's theory of morals which the Theaetetus bears to his theory of knowledge.

(d) A few minor points still remain to be summed up: (1) The extravagant irony in the reason which is assigned for the pilot's modest charge; and in the proposed use of rhetoric as an instrument of self-condemnation; and in the mighty power of geometrical equality in both worlds. (2) The reference of the mythus to the previous discussion should not be overlooked: the fate reserved for incurable criminals such as Archelaus; the retaliation of the box on the ears; the nakedness of the souls and of the judges who are stript of the clothes or disguises which rhetoric and public opinion have hitherto provided for them (compare Swift's notion that the universe is a suit of clothes, Tale of a Tub). The fiction seems to have involved Plato in the necessity of supposing that the soul retained a sort of corporeal likeness after death. (3) The appeal of the authority of Homer, who says that Odysseus saw Minos in his court "holding a golden sceptre," which gives verisimilitude to the tale.

It is scarcely necessary to repeat that Plato is playing "both sides of the game," and that in criticising the characters of Gorgias and Polus, we are not passing any judgment on historical individuals, but only attempting to analyze the "dramatis personae' as they were conceived by him. Neither is it necessary to enlarge upon the obvious fact that Plato is a dramatic writer, whose real opinions cannot always be assumed to be those which he puts into the mouth of Socrates, or any other speaker who appears to have the best of the argument; or to repeat the observation that he is a poet as well as a philosopher; or to remark that he is not to be tried by a modern standard, but interpreted with reference to his place in the history of thought and the opinion of his time.

It has been said that the most characteristic feature of the Gorgias is the assertion of the right of dissent, or private judgment. But this mode of stating the question is really opposed both to the spirit of Plato and of ancient philosophy generally. For Plato is not asserting any abstract right or duty of toleration, or advantage to be derived from freedom of thought; indeed, in some other parts of his writings (e.g., Laws), he has fairly laid himself open to the charge of intolerance. No speculations had as yet arisen respecting the "liberty of prophesying;" and Plato is not affirming any abstract right of this nature: but he is asserting the duty and right of the one wise and true man to dissent from the folly and falsehood of the many. At the same time he acknowledges the natural result, which he hardly seeks to avert, that he who speaks the truth to a multitude, regardless of consequences, will probably share the fate of Socrates.

---

The irony of Plato sometimes veils from us the height of idealism to which he soars. When declaring truths which the many will not receive, he puts on an armour which cannot be pierced by them. The weapons of ridicule are taken out of their hands and the laugh is turned against themselves. The disguises which Socrates assumes are like the parables of the New Testament, or the oracles of the Delphian God; they half conceal, half reveal, his meaning. The more he is in earnest, the more ironical he becomes; and he is never more in earnest or more ironical than in the Gorgias. He hardly troubles himself to answer seriously the objections of Gorgias and Polus, and therefore he sometimes appears to be careless of the ordinary requirements of logic. Yet in the highest sense he is always logical and consistent with himself. The form of the argument may be paradoxical; the substance is an appeal to the higher reason. He is uttering truths before they can be understood, as in all ages the words of philosophers, when they are first uttered, have found the world unprepared for them. A further misunderstanding arises out of the wildness of his humour; he is supposed not only by Callicles, but by the rest of mankind, to be jesting when he is profoundly serious. At length he makes even Polus in earnest. Finally, he drops the argument, and heedless any longer of the forms of dialectic, he loses himself in a sort of triumph, while at the same time he retaliates upon his adversaries. From this confusion of jest and earnest, we may now return to the ideal truth, and draw out in a simple form the main theses of the dialogue.

First Thesis:–

It is a greater evil to do than to suffer injustice.

Compare the New Testament–

"It is better to suffer for well doing than for evil doing."– 1 Pet.

And the Sermon on the Mount–

"Blessed are they that are persecuted for righteousness' sake."–Matt.

The words of Socrates are more abstract than the words of Christ, but they equally imply that the only real evil is moral evil. The righteous may suffer or die, but they have their reward; and even if they had no reward, would be happier than the wicked. The world, represented by Polus, is ready, when they are asked, to acknowledge that injustice is dishonourable, and for their own sakes men are willing to punish the offender (compare Republic). But they are not equally willing to acknowledge that injustice, even if successful, is essentially evil, and has the nature of disease and death. Especially when crimes are committed on the great scale–the crimes of tyrants, ancient or modern–after a while, seeing that they cannot be undone, and have become a part of history, mankind are disposed to forgive them, not from any magnanimity or charity, but because their feelings are blunted by time, and "to forgive is convenient to them." The tangle of good and evil can no longer be unravelled; and although they know that the end cannot justify the means, they feel also that good has often come out of evil. But Socrates would have us pass the same judgment on the tyrant now and always; though he is surrounded by his satellites, and has the applauses of Europe and Asia ringing in his ears; though he is the civilizer or liberator of half a continent, he is, and always will be, the most miserable of men. The greatest consequences for good or for evil cannot alter a hair's breadth the morality of actions which are right or wrong in themselves. This is the standard which Socrates holds up to us. Because politics, and perhaps human life generally, are of a mixed nature we must not allow our principles to sink to the level of our practice.

And so of private individuals–to them, too, the world occasionally speaks of the consequences of their actions:–if they are lovers of pleasure, they will ruin their health; if they are false or dishonest, they will lose their character. But Socrates would speak to them, not of what will be, but of what is–of the present consequence of lowering and degrading the soul. And all higher natures, or perhaps all men everywhere, if they were not tempted by interest or passion, would agree with him–they would rather be the victims than the perpetrators of an act of treachery or of tyranny. Reason tells them that death comes sooner or later to all, and is not so great an evil as an unworthy life, or rather, if rightly regarded, not an evil at all, but to a good man the greatest good. For in all of us there are slumbering ideals of truth and right, which may at any time awaken and develop a new life in us.

Second Thesis:–

It is better to suffer for wrong doing than not to suffer.

There might have been a condition of human life in which the penalty followed at once, and was proportioned to the offence. Moral evil would then be scarcely distinguishable from physical; mankind would avoid vice as they avoid pain or death. But nature, with a view of deepening and enlarging our characters, has for the most part hidden from us the consequences of our actions, and we can only foresee them by an effort of reflection. To awaken in us this habit of reflection is the business of early education, which is continued in maturer years by observation and experience. The spoilt child is in later life said to be unfortunate–he had better have suffered when he was young, and been saved from suffering afterwards. But is not the sovereign equally unfortunate whose education and manner of life are always concealing from him the consequences of his own actions, until at length they are revealed to him in some terrible downfall, which may, perhaps, have been caused not by his own fault? Another illustration is afforded by the pauper and criminal classes, who scarcely reflect at all, except on the means by which they can compass their immediate ends. We pity them, and make allowances for them; but we do not consider that the same principle applies to human actions generally. Not to have been found out in some dishonesty or folly, regarded from a moral or religious point of view, is the greatest of misfortunes. The success of our evil doings is a proof that the gods have ceased to strive with us, and have given us over to ourselves. There is nothing to remind us of our sins, and therefore nothing to correct them. Like our sorrows, they are healed by time;

> *"While rank corruption, mining all within,*
> *Infects unseen."*

The "accustomed irony" of Socrates adds a corollary to the argument:–" Would you punish your enemy, you should allow him to escape unpunished"–this is the true retaliation. (Compare the obscure verse of Proverbs, "Therefore if thine enemy hunger, feed him," etc., quoted in Romans.)

Men are not in the habit of dwelling upon the dark side of their own lives: they do not easily see themselves as others see them. They are very kind and very blind to their own faults; the rhetoric of self-love is always pleading with them on their own behalf. Adopting a similar figure of speech, Socrates would have them use rhetoric, not in defence but in accusation of themselves. As they are guided by feeling rather than by reason, to their feelings the appeal must be made. They must speak to themselves; they must argue with themselves; they must paint in eloquent words the character of their own evil deeds. To any suffering which they have deserved, they must persuade themselves to submit. Under the figure there lurks a real thought, which, expressed in another form, admits of an easy application to ourselves. For do not we too accuse as well as excuse ourselves? And we call to our aid the rhetoric of prayer and preaching, which the mind silently employs while the struggle between the better and the worse is going on within us. And sometimes we are too hard upon ourselves, because we want to restore the balance which self-love has overthrown or disturbed; and then again we may hear a voice as of a parent consoling us. In religious diaries a sort of drama is often enacted by the consciences of men "accusing or else excusing them." For all our life long we are talking with ourselves:–What is thought but speech? What is feeling but rhetoric? And if rhetoric is used on one side only we shall be always in danger of being deceived. And so the words of Socrates, which at first sounded paradoxical, come home to the experience of all of us.

Third Thesis:–

We do not what we will, but what we wish.

Socrates would teach us a lesson which we are slow to learn–that good intentions, and even benevolent actions, when they are not prompted by wisdom, are of no value. We believe something to be for our good which we afterwards find out not to be for our good. The consequences may be inevitable, for they may follow an invariable law, yet they may often be the very opposite of what is expected by us. When we increase pauperism by almsgiving; when we tie up property without regard to changes of circumstances; when we say hastily what we deliberately disapprove; when we do in a moment of passion what upon reflection we regret; when from any want of self-control we give another an advantage over us–we are doing not what we will, but what we wish. All actions of which the consequences are not weighed and foreseen, are of this impotent and paralytic sort; and the author of them has "the least possible power" while seeming to have the greatest. For he is actually bringing about the reverse of what he intended. And yet the book of nature is open to him, in which he who runs may read if he will exercise ordinary attention; every day offers him experiences of his own and of other men's characters, and he passes them unheeded by. The contemplation of the consequences of actions, and the ignorance of men in regard to them, seems to have led Socrates to his famous thesis:–"Virtue is knowledge;" which is not so much an error or paradox as a half truth, seen first in the twilight of ethical philosophy, but also the half of the truth which is especially needed in the present age. For as the world has grown older men have been too apt to imagine a right and wrong apart from consequences; while a few, on the other hand, have sought to resolve them wholly into their consequences. But Socrates, or Plato for him, neither divides nor identifies them; though the time has not yet arrived either for utilitarian or transcendental systems of moral philosophy, he recognizes the two elements which seem to lie at the basis of morality. (Compare the following: "Now, and for us, it is a time to Hellenize and to praise knowing; for we have Hebraized too much and have overvalued doing. But the habits and discipline received from Hebraism remain for our race an eternal possession. And as humanity is constituted, one must never assign the second rank to-day without being ready to restore them to the first to-morrow." Sir William W. Hunter, Preface to Orissa.)

Fourth Thesis:–

To be and not to seem is the end of life.

The Greek in the age of Plato admitted praise to be one of the chief incentives to moral virtue, and to most men the opinion of their fellows is a leading principle of action. Hence a certain element of seeming enters into all things; all or almost all desire to appear better than they are, that they may win the esteem or admiration of others. A man of ability can easily feign the language of piety or virtue; and there is an unconscious as well as a conscious hypocrisy which, according to Socrates, is the worst of the two. Again, there is the sophistry of classes and professions. There are the different opinions about themselves and one another which prevail in different ranks of society. There is the bias given to the mind by the study of one department of human knowledge to the exclusion of the rest; and stronger far the prejudice engendered by a pecuniary or party interest in certain tenets. There is the sophistry of law, the sophistry of medicine, the sophistry of politics, the sophistry of theology. All of these disguises wear the appearance of the truth; some of them are very ancient, and we do not easily disengage ourselves from them; for we have inherited them, and they have become a part of us. The sophistry of an ancient Greek sophist is nothing compared with the sophistry of a religious order, or of a church in which during many ages falsehood has been accumulating, and everything has been said on one side, and nothing on the other. The conventions and customs which we observe in conversation, and the opposition of our interests when we have dealings with one another ("the buyer saith, it is nought–it is nought," etc.), are always obscuring our sense of truth and right. The sophistry of human nature is far more subtle than the deceit of any one man. Few persons speak freely from their own natures, and scarcely any one dares to think for himself: most of us imperceptibly fall into the opinions of those around us, which we partly help to make. A man who would shake himself loose from them, requires great force of mind; he hardly knows where to begin in the search after truth. On every side he is met by the world, which is not an abstraction of theologians, but the most real of all things, being another name for ourselves when regarded collectively and subjected to the influences of society.

Then comes Socrates, impressed as no other man ever was, with the unreality and untruthfulness of popular opinion, and tells mankind that they must be and not seem. How are they to be? At any rate they must have the spirit and desire to be. If they are ignorant, they must acknowledge their ignorance to themselves; if they are conscious of doing evil, they must learn to do well; if they are weak, and have nothing in them which they can call themselves, they must acquire firmness and consistency; if they are indifferent, they must begin to take an interest in the great questions which surround them. They must try to be what they would fain appear in the eyes of their fellow-men. A single individual cannot easily change public opinion; but he can be true and innocent, simple and independent; he can know what he does, and what he does not know; and though not without an effort, he can form a judgment of his own, at least in common matters. In his most secret actions he can show the same high principle (compare Republic) which he shows when supported and watched by public opinion. And on some fitting occasion, on some question of humanity or truth or right, even an ordinary man, from the natural rectitude of his disposition, may be found to take up arms against a whole tribe of politicians and lawyers, and be too much for them.

Who is the true and who the false statesman?–

The true statesman is he who brings order out of disorder; who first organizes and then administers the government of his own country; and having made a nation, seeks to reconcile the national interests with those of Europe and of mankind. He is not a mere theorist, nor yet a dealer in expedients; the whole and the parts grow together in his mind; while the head is conceiving, the hand is executing. Although obliged to descend to the world, he is not of the world. His thoughts are fixed not on power or riches or extension of territory, but on an ideal state, in which all the citizens have an equal chance of health and life, and the highest education is within the reach of all, and the moral and intellectual qualities of every individual are freely developed, and "the idea of good" is the animating principle of the whole. Not the attainment of freedom alone, or of order alone, but how to unite freedom with order is the problem which he has to solve.

The statesman who places before himself these lofty aims has undertaken a task which will call forth all his powers. He must control himself before he can control others; he must know mankind before he can manage them. He has no private likes or dislikes; he does not conceal personal enmity under the disguise of moral or political principle: such meannesses, into which men too often fall unintentionally, are absorbed in the consciousness of his mission, and in his love for his country and for mankind. He will sometimes ask himself what the next generation will say of him; not because he is careful of posthumous fame, but because he knows that the result of his life as a whole will then be more fairly judged. He will take time for the execution of his plans; not hurrying them on when the mind of a nation is unprepared for them; but like the Ruler of the Universe Himself, working in the appointed time, for he knows that human life, "if not long in comparison with eternity" (Republic), is sufficient for the fulfilment of many great purposes. He knows, too, that the work will be still going on when he is no longer here; and he will sometimes, especially when his powers are failing, think of that other "city of which the pattern is in heaven" (Republic).

The false politician is the serving-man of the state. In order to govern men he becomes like them; their "minds are married in conjunction;" they "bear themselves" like vulgar and tyrannical masters, and he is their obedient servant. The true politician, if he would rule men, must make them like himself; he must "educate his party" until they cease to be a party; he must breathe into them the spirit which will hereafter give form to their institutions. Politics with him are not a mechanism for seeming what he is not, or for carrying out the will of the majority. Himself a representative man, he is the representative not of the lower but of the higher elements of the nation. There is a better (as well as a worse) public opinion of which he seeks to lay hold; as there is also a deeper current of human affairs in which he is borne up when the waves nearer the shore are threatening him. He acknowledges that he cannot take the world by force–two or three moves on the political chess board are all that he can fore see–two or three weeks moves on the political chessboard are all that he can foresee–two or three weeks or months are granted to him in which he can provide against a coming struggle. But he knows also that there are permanent principles of politics which are always tending to the well-being of states–better administration, better education, the reconciliation of conflicting elements, increased security against external enemies. These are not "of to-day or yesterday," but are the same in all times, and under all forms of government. Then when the storm descends and the winds blow, though he knows not beforehand the hour of danger, the pilot, not like Plato's captain in the Republic, half-blind and deaf, but with penetrating eye and quick ear, is ready to take command of the ship and guide her into port.

The false politician asks not what is true, but what is the opinion of the world–not what is right, but what is expedient. The only measures of which he approves are the measures which will pass. He has no intention of fighting an uphill battle; he keeps the roadway of politics. He is unwilling to incur the persecution and enmity which political convictions would entail upon him. He begins with popularity, and in fair weather sails gallantly along. But unpopularity soon follows him. For men expect their leaders to be better and wiser than themselves: to be their guides in danger, their saviours in extremity; they do not really desire them to obey all the ignorant impulses of the popular mind; and if they fail them in a crisis they are disappointed. Then, as Socrates says, the cry of ingratitude is heard, which is most unreasonable; for the people, who have been taught no better, have done what might be expected of them, and their statesmen have received justice at their hands.

The true statesman is aware that he must adapt himself to times and circumstances. He must have allies if he is to fight against the world; he must enlighten public opinion; he must accustom his followers to act together. Although he is not the mere executor of the will of the majority, he must win over the majority to himself. He is their leader and not their follower, but in order to lead he must also follow. He will neither exaggerate nor undervalue the power of a statesman, neither adopting the "laissez faire" nor the "paternal government" principle; but he will, whether he is dealing with children in politics, or with full-grown men, seek to do for the people what the government can do for them, and what, from imperfect education or deficient powers of combination, they cannot do for themselves. He knows that if he does too much for them they will do nothing; and that if he does nothing for them they will in some states of society be utterly helpless. For the many cannot exist without the few, if the material force of a country is from below, wisdom and experience are from above. It is not a small part of human evils which kings and governments make or cure. The statesman is well aware that a great purpose carried out consistently during many years will at last be executed. He is playing for a stake which may be partly determined by some accident, and therefore he will allow largely for the unknown element of politics. But the game being one in which chance and skill are combined, if he plays long enough he is certain of victory. He will not be always consistent, for the world is changing; and though he depends upon the support of a party, he will remember that he is the minister of the whole. He lives not for the present, but for the future, and he is not at all sure that he will be appreciated either now or then. For he may have the existing order of society against him, and may not be remembered by a distant posterity.

There are always discontented idealists in politics who, like Socrates in the Gorgias, find fault with all statesmen past as well as present, not excepting the greatest names of history. Mankind have an uneasy feeling that they ought to be better governed than they are. Just as the actual philosopher falls short of the one wise man, so does the actual statesman fall short of the ideal. And so partly from vanity and egotism, but partly also from a true sense of the faults of eminent men, a temper of dissatisfaction and criticism springs up among those who are ready enough to acknowledge the inferiority of their own powers. No matter whether a statesman makes high professions or none at all–they are reduced sooner or later to the same level. And sometimes the more unscrupulous man is better esteemed than the more conscientious, because he has not equally deceived expectations. Such sentiments may be unjust, but they are widely spread; we constantly find them recurring in reviews and newspapers, and still oftener in private conversation.

We may further observe that the art of government, while in some respects tending to improve, has in others a tendency to degenerate, as institutions become more popular. Governing for the people cannot easily be combined with governing by the people: the interests of classes are too strong for the ideas of the statesman who takes a comprehensive view of the whole. According to Socrates the true governor will find ruin or death staring him in the face, and will only be induced to govern from the fear of being governed by a worse man than himself (Republic). And in modern times, though the world has grown milder, and the terrible consequences which Plato foretells no longer await an English statesman, any one who is not actuated by a blind ambition will only undertake from a sense of duty a work in which he is most likely to fail; and even if he succeed, will rarely be rewarded by the gratitude of his own generation.

Socrates, who is not a politician at all, tells us that he is the only real politician of his time. Let us illustrate the meaning of his words by applying them to the history of our own country. He would have said that not Pitt or Fox, or Canning or Sir R. Peel, are the real politicians of their time, but Locke, Hume, Adam Smith, Bentham, Ricardo. These during the greater part of their lives occupied an inconsiderable space in the eyes of the public. They were private persons; nevertheless they sowed in the minds of men seeds which in the next generation have become an irresistible power. "Herein is that saying true, One soweth and another reapeth." We may imagine with Plato an ideal statesman in whom practice and speculation are perfectly harmonized; for there is no necessary opposition between them. But experience shows that they are commonly divorced–the ordinary politician is the interpreter or executor of the thoughts of others, and hardly ever brings to the birth a new political conception. One or two only in modern times, like the Italian statesman Cavour, have created the world in which they moved. The philosopher is naturally unfitted for political life; his great ideas are not understood by the many; he is a thousand miles away from the questions of the day. Yet perhaps the lives of thinkers, as they are stiller and deeper, are also happier than the lives of those who are more in the public eye. They have the promise of the future, though they are regarded as dreamers and visionaries by their own contemporaries. And when they are no longer here, those who would have been ashamed of them during their lives claim kindred with them, and are proud to be called by their names. (Compare Thucyd.)

Who is the true poet?

Plato expels the poets from his Republic because they are allied to sense; because they stimulate the emotions; because they are thrice removed from the ideal truth. And in a similar spirit he declares in the Gorgias that the stately muse of tragedy is a votary of pleasure and not of truth. In modern times we almost ridicule the idea of poetry admitting of a moral. The poet and the prophet, or preacher, in primitive antiquity are one and the same; but in later ages they seem to fall apart. The great art of novel writing, that peculiar creation of our own and the last century, which, together with the sister art of review writing, threatens to absorb all literature, has even less of seriousness in her composition. Do we not often hear the novel writer censured for attempting to convey a lesson to the minds of his readers?

Yet the true office of a poet or writer of fiction is not merely to give amusement, or to be the expression of the feelings of mankind, good or bad, or even to increase our knowledge of human nature. There have been poets in modern times, such as Goethe or Wordsworth, who have not forgotten their high vocation of teachers; and the two greatest of the Greek dramatists owe their sublimity to their ethical character. The noblest truths, sung of in the purest and sweetest language, are still the proper material of poetry. The poet clothes them with beauty, and has a power of making them enter into the hearts and memories of men. He has not only to speak of themes above the level of ordinary life, but to speak of them in a deeper and tenderer way than they are ordinarily felt, so as to awaken the feeling of them in others. The old he makes young again; the familiar principle he invests with a new dignity; he finds a noble expression for the common-places of morality and politics. He uses the things of sense so as to indicate what is beyond; he raises us through earth to heaven. He expresses what the better part of us would fain say, and the half-conscious feeling is strengthened by the expression. He is his own critic, for the spirit of poetry and of criticism are not divided in him. His mission is not to disguise men from themselves, but to reveal to them their own nature, and make them better acquainted with the world around them. True poetry is the remembrance of youth, of love, the embodiment in words of the happiest and holiest moments of life, of the noblest thoughts of man, of the greatest deeds of the past. The poet of the future may return to his greater calling of the prophet or teacher; indeed, we hardly know what may not be effected for the human race by a better use of the poetical and imaginative faculty. The reconciliation of poetry, as of religion, with truth, may still be possible. Neither is the element of pleasure to be excluded. For when we substitute a higher pleasure for a lower we raise men in the scale of existence. Might not the novelist, too, make an ideal, or rather many ideals of social life, better than a thousand sermons? Plato, like the Puritans, is too much afraid of poetic and artistic influences. But he is not without a true sense of the noble purposes to which art may be applied (Republic).

Modern poetry is often a sort of plaything, or, in Plato's language, a flattery, a sophistry, or sham, in which, without any serious purpose, the poet lends wings to his fancy and exhibits his gifts of language and metre. Such an one seeks to gratify the taste of his readers; he has the "savoir faire," or trick of writing, but he has not the higher spirit of poetry. He has no conception that true art should bring order out of disorder; that it should make provision for the soul's highest interest; that it should be pursued only with a view to "the improvement of the citizens." He ministers to the weaker side of human nature (Republic); he idealizes the sensual; he sings the strain of love in the latest fashion; instead of raising men above themselves he brings them back to the "tyranny of the many masters," from which all his life long a good man has been praying to be delivered. And often, forgetful of measure and order, he will express not that which is truest, but that which is strongest. Instead of a great and nobly-executed subject, perfect in every part, some fancy of a heated brain is worked out with the strangest incongruity. He is not the master of his words, but his words–perhaps borrowed from another–the faded reflection of some French or German or Italian writer, have the better of him. Though we are not going to banish the poets, how can we suppose that such utterances have any healing or life-giving influence on the minds of men?

"Let us hear the conclusion of the whole matter:" Art then must be true, and politics must be true, and the life of man must be true and not a seeming or sham. In all of them order has to be brought out of disorder, truth out of error and falsehood. This is what we mean by the greatest improvement of man. And so, having considered in what way "we can best spend the appointed time, we leave the result with God." Plato does not say that God will order all things for the best (compare Phaedo), but he indirectly implies that the evils of this life will be corrected in another. And as we are very far from the best imaginable world at present, Plato here, as in the Phaedo and Republic, supposes a purgatory or place of education for mankind in general, and for a very few a Tartarus or hell. The myth which terminates the dialogue is not the revelation, but rather, like all similar descriptions, whether in the Bible or Plato, the veil of another life. For no visible thing can reveal the invisible. Of this Plato, unlike some commentators on Scripture, is fully aware. Neither will he dogmatize about the manner in which we are "born again" (Republic). Only he is prepared to maintain the ultimate triumph of truth and right, and declares that no one, not even the wisest of the Greeks, can affirm any other doctrine without being ridiculous.

There is a further paradox of ethics, in which pleasure and pain are held to be indifferent, and virtue at the time of action and without regard to consequences is happiness. From this elevation or exaggeration of feeling Plato seems to shrink: he leaves it to the Stoics in a later generation to maintain that when impaled or on the rack the philosopher may be happy (compare Republic). It is observable that in the Republic he raises this question, but it is not really discussed; the veil of the ideal state, the shadow of another life, are allowed to descend upon it and it passes out of sight. The martyr or sufferer in the cause of right or truth is often supposed to die in raptures, having his eye fixed on a city which is in heaven. But if there were no future, might he not still be happy in the performance of an action which was attended only by a painful death? He himself may be ready to thank God that he was thought worthy to do Him the least service, without looking for a reward; the joys of another life may not have been present to his mind at all. Do we suppose that the mediaeval saint, St. Bernard, St. Francis, St. Catharine of Sienna, or the Catholic priest who lately devoted himself to death by a lingering disease that he might solace and help others, was thinking of the "sweets" of heaven? No; the work was already heaven to him and enough. Much less will the dying patriot be dreaming of the praises of man or of an immortality of fame: the sense of duty, of right, and trust in God will be sufficient, and as far as the mind can reach, in that hour. If he were certain that there were no life to come, he would not have wished to speak or act otherwise than he did in the cause of truth or of humanity. Neither, on the other hand, will he suppose that God has forsaken him or that the future is to be a mere blank to him. The greatest act of faith, the only faith which cannot pass away, is his who has not known, but yet has believed. A very few among the sons of men have made themselves independent of circumstances, past, present, or to come. He who has attained to such a temper of mind has already present with him eternal life; he needs no arguments to convince him of immortality; he has in him already a principle stronger than death. He who serves man without the thought of reward is deemed to be a more faithful servant than he who works for hire. May not the service of God, which is the more disinterested, be in like manner the higher? And although only a very few in the course of the world's history–Christ himself being one of them–have attained to such a noble conception of God and of the human soul, yet the ideal of them may be present to us, and the remembrance of them be an example to us, and their lives may shed a light on many dark places both of philosophy and theology.

THE MYTHS OF PLATO.

The myths of Plato are a phenomenon unique in literature. There are four longer ones: these occur in the Phaedrus, Phaedo, Gorgias, and Republic. That in the Republic is the most elaborate and finished of them. Three of these greater myths, namely those contained in the Phaedo, the Gorgias and the Republic, relate to the destiny of human souls in a future life. The magnificent myth in the Phaedrus treats of the immortality, or rather the eternity of the soul, in which is included a former as well as a future state of existence. To these may be added, (1) the myth, or rather fable, occurring in the Statesman, in which the life of innocence is contrasted with the ordinary life of man and the consciousness of evil: (2) the legend of the Island of Atlantis, an imaginary history, which is a fragment only, commenced in the Timaeus and continued in the Critias: (3) the much less artistic fiction of the foundation of the Cretan colony which is introduced in the preface to the Laws, but soon falls into the background: (4) the beautiful but rather artificial tale of Prometheus and Epimetheus narrated in his rhetorical manner by Protagoras in the dialogue called after him: (5) the speech at the beginning of the Phaedrus, which is a parody of the orator Lysias; the rival speech of Socrates and the recantation of it. To these may be added (6) the tale of the grasshoppers, and (7) the tale of Thamus and of Theuth, both in the Phaedrus: (8) the parable of the Cave (Republic), in which the previous argument is recapitulated, and the nature and degrees of knowledge having been previously set forth in the abstract are represented in a picture: (9) the fiction of the earth-born men (Republic; compare Laws), in which by the adaptation of an old tradition Plato makes a new beginning for his society: (10) the myth of Aristophanes respecting the division of the sexes, Sym.: (11) the parable of the noble captain, the pilot, and the mutinous sailors (Republic), in which is represented the relation of the better part of the world, and of the philosopher, to the mob of politicians: (12) the ironical tale of the pilot who plies between Athens and Aegina charging only a small payment for saving men from death, the reason being that he is uncertain whether to live or die is better for them (Gor.): (13) the treatment of freemen and citizens by physicians and of slaves by their apprentices,–a somewhat laboured figure of speech intended to illustrate the two different ways in which the laws speak to men (Laws). There also occur in Plato continuous images; some of them extend over several pages, appearing and reappearing at intervals: such as the bees stinging and stingless (paupers and thieves) in the Eighth Book of the Republic, who are generated in the transition from timocracy to oligarchy: the sun, which is to the visible world what the idea of good is to the intellectual, in the Sixth Book of the Republic: the composite animal, having the form of a man, but containing under a human skin a lion and a many-headed monster (Republic): the great beast, i.e. the populace: and the wild beast within us, meaning the passions which are always liable to break out: the animated comparisons of the degradation of philosophy by the arts to the dishonoured maiden, and of the tyrant to the parricide, who "beats his father, having first taken away his arms": the dog, who is your only philosopher: the grotesque and rather paltry image of the argument wandering about without a head (Laws), which is repeated, not improved, from the Gorgias: the argument personified as veiling her face (Republic), as engaged in a chase, as breaking upon us in a first, second and third wave:–on these figures of speech the changes are rung many times over. It is observable that nearly all these parables or continuous images are found in the Republic; that which occurs in the Theaetetus, of the midwifery of Socrates, is perhaps the only exception. To make the list complete, the mathematical figure of the number of the state (Republic), or the numerical interval which separates king from tyrant, should not be forgotten.

The myth in the Gorgias is one of those descriptions of another life which, like the Sixth Aeneid of Virgil, appear to contain reminiscences of the mysteries. It is a vision of the rewards and punishments which await good and bad men after death. It supposes the body to continue and to be in another world what it has become in this. It includes a Paradiso, Purgatorio, and Inferno, like the sister myths of the Phaedo and the Republic. The Inferno is reserved for great criminals only. The argument of the dialogue is frequently referred to, and the meaning breaks through so as rather to destroy the liveliness and consistency of the picture. The structure of the fiction is very slight, the chief point or moral being that in the judgments of another world there is no possibility of concealment: Zeus has taken from men the power of foreseeing death, and brings together the souls both of them and their judges naked and undisguised at the judgment-seat. Both are exposed to view, stripped of the veils and clothes which might prevent them from seeing into or being seen by one another.

The myth of the Phaedo is of the same type, but it is more cosmological, and also more poetical. The beautiful and ingenious fancy occurs to Plato that the upper atmosphere is an earth and heaven in one, a glorified earth, fairer and purer than that in which we dwell. As the fishes live in the ocean, mankind are living in a lower sphere, out of which they put their heads for a moment or two and behold a world beyond. The earth which we inhabit is a sediment of the coarser particles which drop from the world above, and is to that heavenly earth what the desert and the shores of the ocean are to us. A part of the myth consists of description of the interior of the earth, which gives the opportunity of introducing several mythological names and of providing places of torment for the wicked. There is no clear distinction of soul and body; the spirits beneath the earth are spoken of as souls only, yet they retain a sort of shadowy form when they cry for mercy on the shores of the lake; and the philosopher alone is said to have got rid of the body. All the three myths in Plato which relate to the world below have a place for repentant sinners, as well as other homes or places for the very good and very bad. It is a natural reflection which is made by Plato elsewhere, that the two extremes of human character are rarely met with, and that the generality of mankind are between them. Hence a place must be found for them. In the myth of the Phaedo they are carried down the river Acheron to the Acherusian lake, where they dwell, and are purified of their evil deeds, and receive the rewards of their good. There are also incurable sinners, who are cast into Tartarus, there to remain as the penalty of atrocious crimes; these suffer everlastingly. And there is another class of hardly-curable sinners who are allowed from time to time to approach the shores of the Acherusian lake, where they cry to their victims for mercy; which if they obtain they come out into the lake and cease from their torments.

Neither this, nor any of the three greater myths of Plato, nor perhaps any allegory or parable relating to the unseen world, is consistent with itself. The language of philosophy mingles with that of mythology; abstract ideas are transformed into persons, figures of speech into realities. These myths may be compared with the Pilgrim's Progress of Bunyan, in which discussions of theology are mixed up with the incidents of travel, and mythological personages are associated with human beings: they are also garnished with names and phrases taken out of Homer, and with other fragments of Greek tradition.

The myth of the Republic is more subtle and also more consistent than either of the two others. It has a greater verisimilitude than they have, and is full of touches which recall the experiences of human life. It will be noticed by an attentive reader that the twelve days during which Er lay in a trance after he was slain coincide with the time passed by the spirits in their pilgrimage. It is a curious observation, not often made, that good men who have lived in a well-governed city (shall we say in a religious and respectable society?) are more likely to make mistakes in their choice of life than those who have had more experience of the world and of evil. It is a more familiar remark that we constantly blame others when we have only ourselves to blame; and the philosopher must acknowledge, however reluctantly, that there is an element of chance in human life with which it is sometimes impossible for man to cope. That men drink more of the waters of forgetfulness than is good for them is a poetical description of a familiar truth. We have many of us known men who, like Odysseus, have wearied of ambition and have only desired rest. We should like to know what became of the infants "dying almost as soon as they were born," but Plato only raises, without satisfying, our curiosity. The two companies of souls, ascending and descending at either chasm of heaven and earth, and conversing when they come out into the meadow, the majestic figures of the judges sitting in heaven, the voice heard by Ardiaeus, are features of the great allegory which have an indescribable grandeur and power. The remark already made respecting the inconsistency of the two other myths must be extended also to this: it is at once an orrery, or model of the heavens, and a picture of the Day of Judgment.

The three myths are unlike anything else in Plato. There is an Oriental, or rather an Egyptian element in them, and they have an affinity to the mysteries and to the Orphic modes of worship. To a certain extent they are un-Greek; at any rate there is hardly anything like them in other Greek writings which have a serious purpose; in spirit they are mediaeval. They are akin to what may be termed the underground religion in all ages and countries. They are presented in the most lively and graphic manner, but they are never insisted on as true; it is only affirmed that nothing better can be said about a future life. Plato seems to make use of them when he has reached the limits of human knowledge; or, to borrow an expression of his own, when he is standing on the outside of the intellectual world. They are very simple in style; a few touches bring the picture home to the mind, and make it present to us. They have also a kind of authority gained by the employment of sacred and familiar names, just as mere fragments of the words of Scripture, put together in any form and applied to any subject, have a power of their own. They are a substitute for poetry and mythology; and they are also a reform of mythology. The moral of them may be summed up in a word or two: After death the Judgment; and "there is some better thing remaining for the good than for the evil."

All literature gathers into itself many elements of the past: for example, the tale of the earth-born men in the Republic appears at first sight to be an extravagant fancy, but it is restored to propriety when we remember that it is based on a legendary belief. The art of making stories of ghosts and apparitions credible is said to consist in the manner of telling them. The effect is gained by many literary and conversational devices, such as the previous raising of curiosity, the mention of little circumstances, simplicity, picturesqueness, the naturalness of the occasion, and the like. This art is possessed by Plato in a degree which has never been equalled.

The myth in the Phaedrus is even greater than the myths which have been already described, but is of a different character. It treats of a former rather than of a future life. It represents the conflict of reason aided by passion or righteous indignation on the one hand, and of the animal lusts and instincts on the other. The soul of man has followed the company of some god, and seen truth in the form of the universal before it was born in this world. Our present life is the result of the struggle which was then carried on. This world is relative to a former world, as it is often projected into a future. We ask the question, Where were men before birth? As we likewise enquire, What will become of them after death? The first question is unfamiliar to us, and therefore seems to be unnatural; but if we survey the whole human race, it has been as influential and as widely spread as the other. In the Phaedrus it is really a figure of speech in which the "spiritual combat" of this life is represented. The majesty and power of the whole passage–especially of what may be called the theme or proem (beginning "The mind through all her being is immortal")–can only be rendered very inadequately in another language.

The myth in the Statesman relates to a former cycle of existence, in which men were born of the earth, and by the reversal of the earth's motion had their lives reversed and were restored to youth and beauty: the dead came to life, the old grew middle-aged, and the middle-aged young; the youth became a child, the child an infant, the infant vanished into the earth. The connection between the reversal of the earth's motion and the reversal of human life is of course verbal only, yet Plato, like theologians in other ages, argues from the consistency of the tale to its truth. The new order of the world was immediately under the government of God; it was a state of innocence in which men had neither wants nor cares, in which the earth brought forth all things spontaneously, and God was to man what man now is to the animals. There were no great estates, or families, or private possessions, nor any traditions of the past, because men were all born out of the earth. This is what Plato calls the "reign of Cronos;" and in like manner he connects the reversal of the earth's motion with some legend of which he himself was probably the inventor.

The question is then asked, under which of these two cycles of existence was man the happier,–under that of

Cronos, which was a state of innocence, or that of Zeus, which is our ordinary life? For a while Plato balances the two sides of the serious controversy, which he has suggested in a figure. The answer depends on another question: What use did the children of Cronos make of their time? They had boundless leisure and the faculty of discoursing, not only with one another, but with the animals. Did they employ these advantages with a view to philosophy, gathering from every nature some addition to their store of knowledge? or, Did they pass their time in eating and drinking and telling stories to one another and to the beasts?–in either case there would be no difficulty in answering. But then, as Plato rather mischievously adds, "Nobody knows what they did," and therefore the doubt must remain undetermined.

To the first there succeeds a second epoch. After another natural convulsion, in which the order of the world and of human life is once more reversed, God withdraws his guiding hand, and man is left to the government of himself. The world begins again, and arts and laws are slowly and painfully invented. A secular age succeeds to a theocratical. In this fanciful tale Plato has dropped, or almost dropped, the garb of mythology. He suggests several curious and important thoughts, such as the possibility of a state of innocence, the existence of a world without traditions, and the difference between human and divine government. He has also carried a step further his speculations concerning the abolition of the family and of property, which he supposes to have no place among the children of Cronos any more than in the ideal state.

It is characteristic of Plato and of his age to pass from the abstract to the concrete, from poetry to reality. Language is the expression of the seen, and also of the unseen, and moves in a region between them. A great writer knows how to strike both these chords, sometimes remaining within the sphere of the visible, and then again comprehending a wider range and soaring to the abstract and universal. Even in the same sentence he may employ both modes of speech not improperly or inharmoniously. It is useless to criticise the broken metaphors of Plato, if the effect of the whole is to create a picture not such as can be painted on canvas, but which is full of life and meaning to the reader. A poem may be contained in a word or two, which may call up not one but many latent images; or half reveal to us by a sudden flash the thoughts of many hearts. Often the rapid transition from one image to another is pleasing to us: on the other hand, any single figure of speech if too often repeated, or worked out too much at length, becomes prosy and monotonous. In theology and philosophy we necessarily include both "the moral law within and the starry heaven above," and pass from one to the other (compare for examples Psalms xviii. and xix.). Whether such a use of language is puerile or noble depends upon the genius of the writer or speaker, and the familiarity of the associations employed.

In the myths and parables of Plato the ease and grace of conversation is not forgotten: they are spoken, not written words, stories which are told to a living audience, and so well told that we are more than half-inclined to believe them (compare Phaedrus). As in conversation too, the striking image or figure of speech is not forgotten, but is quickly caught up, and alluded to again and again; as it would still be in our own day in a genial and sympathetic society. The descriptions of Plato have a greater life and reality than is to be found in any modern writing. This is due to their homeliness and simplicity. Plato can do with words just as he pleases; to him they are indeed "more plastic than wax" (Republic). We are in the habit of opposing speech and writing, poetry and prose. But he has discovered a use of language in which they are united; which gives a fitting expression to the highest truths; and in which the trifles of courtesy and the familiarities of daily life are not overlooked.

# GORGIAS

Translated by Benjamin Jowett

PERSONS OF THE DIALOGUE: Callicles, Socrates, Chaerephon, Gorgias, Polus.

SCENE: The house of Callicles.

CALLICLES: The wise man, as the proverb says, is late for a fray, but not for a feast.

SOCRATES: And are we late for a feast?

CALLICLES: Yes, and a delightful feast; for Gorgias has just been exhibiting to us many fine things.

SOCRATES: It is not my fault, Callicles; our friend Chaerephon is to blame; for he would keep us loitering in the Agora.

CHAEREPHON: Never mind, Socrates; the misfortune of which I have been the cause I will also repair; for Gorgias is a friend of mine, and I will make him give the exhibition again either now, or, if you prefer, at some other time.

CALLICLES: What is the matter, Chaerephon–does Socrates want to hear Gorgias?

CHAEREPHON: Yes, that was our intention in coming.

CALLICLES: Come into my house, then; for Gorgias is staying with me, and he shall exhibit to you.

SOCRATES: Very good, Callicles; but will he answer our questions? for I want to hear from him what is the nature of his art, and what it is which he professes and teaches; he may, as you (Chaerephon) suggest, defer the exhibition to some other time.

CALLICLES: There is nothing like asking him, Socrates; and indeed to answer questions is a part of his exhibition, for he was saying only just now, that any one in my house might put any question to him, and that he would answer.

SOCRATES: How fortunate! will you ask him, Chaerephon–?

CHAEREPHON: What shall I ask him?

SOCRATES: Ask him who he is.

CHAEREPHON: What do you mean?

SOCRATES: I mean such a question as would elicit from him, if he had been a maker of shoes, the answer that he is a cobbler. Do you understand?

CHAEREPHON: I understand, and will ask him: Tell me, Gorgias, is our friend Callicles right in saying that you undertake to answer any questions which you are asked?

GORGIAS: Quite right, Chaerephon: I was saying as much only just now; and I may add, that many years have elapsed since any one has asked me a new one.

CHAEREPHON: Then you must be very ready, Gorgias.

GORGIAS: Of that, Chaerephon, you can make trial.

POLUS: Yes, indeed, and if you like, Chaerephon, you may make trial of me too, for I think that Gorgias, who has been talking a long time, is tired.

CHAEREPHON: And do you, Polus, think that you can answer better than Gorgias?

POLUS: What does that matter if I answer well enough for you?

CHAEREPHON: Not at all:–and you shall answer if you like.

POLUS: Ask:–

CHAEREPHON: My question is this: If Gorgias had the skill of his brother Herodicus, what ought we to call him? Ought he not to have the name which is given to his brother?

POLUS: Certainly.

CHAEREPHON: Then we should be right in calling him a physician?

POLUS: Yes.

CHAEREPHON: And if he had the skill of Aristophon the son of Aglaophon, or of his brother Polygnotus, what ought we to call him?

POLUS: Clearly, a painter.

CHAEREPHON: But now what shall we call him–what is the art in which he is skilled.

POLUS: O Chaerephon, there are many arts among mankind which are experimental, and have their origin in experience, for experience makes the days of men to proceed according to art, and inexperience according to chance, and different persons in different ways are proficient in different arts, and the best persons in the best arts. And our friend Gorgias is one of the best, and the art in which he is a proficient is the noblest.

SOCRATES: Polus has been taught how to make a capital speech, Gorgias; but he is not fulfilling the promise which he made to Chaerephon.

GORGIAS: What do you mean, Socrates?

SOCRATES: I mean that he has not exactly answered the question which he was asked.

GORGIAS: Then why not ask him yourself?

SOCRATES: But I would much rather ask you, if you are disposed to answer: for I see, from the few words which Polus has uttered, that he has attended more to the art which is called rhetoric than to dialectic.

POLUS: What makes you say so, Socrates?

SOCRATES: Because, Polus, when Chaerephon asked you what was the art which Gorgias knows, you praised it as if you were answering some one who found fault with it, but you never said what the art was.

POLUS: Why, did I not say that it was the noblest of arts?

SOCRATES: Yes, indeed, but that was no answer to the question: nobody asked what was the quality, but what was the nature, of the art, and by what name we were to describe Gorgias. And I would still beg you briefly and clearly, as you answered Chaerephon when he asked you at first, to say what this art is, and what we ought to call Gorgias: Or rather, Gorgias, let me turn to you, and ask the same question,–what are we to call you, and what is the art which you profess?

GORGIAS: Rhetoric, Socrates, is my art.

SOCRATES: Then I am to call you a rhetorician?

GORGIAS: Yes, Socrates, and a good one too, if you would call me that which, in Homeric language, "I boast myself to be."

SOCRATES: I should wish to do so.

GORGIAS: Then pray do.

SOCRATES: And are we to say that you are able to make other men rhetoricians?

GORGIAS: Yes, that is exactly what I profess to make them, not only at Athens, but in all places.

SOCRATES: And will you continue to ask and answer questions, Gorgias, as we are at present doing, and reserve for another occasion the longer mode of speech which Polus was attempting? Will you keep your promise, and answer shortly the questions which are asked of you?

GORGIAS: Some answers, Socrates, are of necessity longer; but I will do my best to make them as short as possible; for a part of my profession is that I can be as short as any one.

SOCRATES: That is what is wanted, Gorgias; exhibit the shorter method now, and the longer one at some other time.

GORGIAS: Well, I will; and you will certainly say, that you never heard a man use fewer words.

SOCRATES: Very good then; as you profess to be a rhetorician, and a maker of rhetoricians, let me ask you, with what is rhetoric concerned: I might ask with what is weaving concerned, and you would reply (would you not?), with the making of garments?

GORGIAS: Yes.

SOCRATES: And music is concerned with the composition of melodies?

GORGIAS: It is.

SOCRATES: By Here, Gorgias, I admire the surpassing brevity of your answers.

GORGIAS: Yes, Socrates, I do think myself good at that.

SOCRATES: I am glad to hear it; answer me in like manner about rhetoric: with what is rhetoric concerned?

GORGIAS: With discourse.

SOCRATES: What sort of discourse, Gorgias?–such discourse as would teach the sick under what treatment they might get well?

GORGIAS: No.

SOCRATES: Then rhetoric does not treat of all kinds of discourse?

GORGIAS: Certainly not.

SOCRATES: And yet rhetoric makes men able to speak?

GORGIAS: Yes.

SOCRATES: And to understand that about which they speak?

GORGIAS: Of course.

SOCRATES: But does not the art of medicine, which we were just now mentioning, also make men able to understand and speak about the sick?

GORGIAS: Certainly.

SOCRATES: Then medicine also treats of discourse?

GORGIAS: Yes.

SOCRATES: Of discourse concerning diseases?

GORGIAS: Just so.

SOCRATES: And does not gymnastic also treat of discourse concerning the good or evil condition of the body?

GORGIAS: Very true.

SOCRATES: And the same, Gorgias, is true of the other arts:–all of them treat of discourse concerning the subjects with which they severally have to do.

GORGIAS: Clearly.

SOCRATES: Then why, if you call rhetoric the art which treats of discourse, and all the other arts treat of discourse, do you not call them arts of rhetoric?

GORGIAS: Because, Socrates, the knowledge of the other arts has only to do with some sort of external action, as of the hand; but there is no such action of the hand in rhetoric which works and takes effect only through the medium of discourse. And therefore I am justified in saying that rhetoric treats of discourse.

SOCRATES: I am not sure whether I entirely understand you, but I dare say I shall soon know better; please to answer me a question:–you would allow that there are arts?

GORGIAS: Yes.

SOCRATES: As to the arts generally, they are for the most part concerned with doing, and require little or no speaking; in painting, and statuary, and many other arts, the work may proceed in silence; and of such arts I suppose you would say that they do not come within the province of rhetoric.

GORGIAS: You perfectly conceive my meaning, Socrates.

SOCRATES: But there are other arts which work wholly through the medium of language, and require either no action or very little, as, for example, the arts of arithmetic, of calculation, of geometry, and of playing draughts; in some of these speech is pretty nearly co-extensive with action, but in most of them the verbal element is greater–they depend wholly on words for their efficacy and power: and I take your meaning to be that rhetoric is an art of this latter sort?

GORGIAS: Exactly.

SOCRATES: And yet I do not believe that you really mean to call any of these arts rhetoric; although the precise expression which you used was, that rhetoric is an art which works and takes effect only through the medium of discourse; and an adversary who wished to be captious might say, "And so, Gorgias, you call arithmetic rhetoric." But I do not think that you really call arithmetic rhetoric any more than geometry would be so called by you.

GORGIAS: You are quite right, Socrates, in your apprehension of my meaning.

SOCRATES: Well, then, let me now have the rest of my answer:–seeing that rhetoric is one of those arts which works mainly by the use of words, and there are other arts which also use words, tell me what is that quality in words with which rhetoric is concerned:–Suppose that a person asks me about some of the arts which I was mentioning just now; he might say, "Socrates, what is arithmetic?" and I should reply to him, as you replied to me, that arithmetic is one of those arts which take effect through words. And then he would proceed to ask: "Words about what?" and I should reply, Words about odd and even numbers, and how many there are of each. And if he asked again: "What is the art of calculation?" I should say, That also is one of the arts which is concerned wholly with words. And if he further said, "Concerned with what?" I should say, like the clerks in the assembly, "as aforesaid" of arithmetic, but with a difference, the difference being that the art of calculation considers not only the quantities of odd and even numbers, but also their numerical relations to themselves and to one another. And suppose, again, I were to say that astronomy is only words–he would ask, "Words about what, Socrates?" and I should answer, that astronomy tells us about the motions of the stars and sun and moon, and their relative swiftness.

GORGIAS: You would be quite right, Socrates.

SOCRATES: And now let us have from you, Gorgias, the truth about rhetoric: which you would admit (would you not?) to be one of those arts which act always and fulfil all their ends through the medium of words?

GORGIAS: True.

SOCRATES: Words which do what? I should ask. To what class of things do the words which rhetoric uses relate?

GORGIAS: To the greatest, Socrates, and the best of human things.

SOCRATES: That again, Gorgias is ambiguous; I am still in the dark: for which are the greatest and best of human things? I dare say that you have heard men singing at feasts the old drinking song, in which the singers enumerate the goods of life, first health, beauty next, thirdly, as the writer of the song says, wealth honestly obtained.

GORGIAS: Yes, I know the song; but what is your drift?

SOCRATES: I mean to say, that the producers of those things which the author of the song praises, that is to say, the physician, the trainer, the money-maker, will at once come to you, and first the physician will say: "O Socrates, Gorgias is deceiving you, for my art is concerned with the greatest good of men and not his." And when I ask, Who are you? he will reply, "I am a physician." What do you mean? I shall say. Do you mean that your art produces the greatest good? "Certainly," he will answer, "for is not health the greatest good? What greater good can men have, Socrates?" And after him the trainer will come and say, "I too, Socrates, shall be greatly surprised if Gorgias can show more good of his art than I can show of mine." To him again I shall say, Who are you, honest friend, and what is your business? "I am a trainer," he will reply, "and my business is to make men beautiful and strong in body." When I have done with the trainer, there arrives the money-maker, and he, as I expect, will utterly despise them all. "Consider Socrates," he will say, "whether Gorgias or any one else can produce any greater good than wealth." Well, you and I say to him, and are you a creator of wealth? "Yes," he replies. And who are you? "A money-maker." And do you consider wealth to be the greatest good of man? "Of course," will be his reply. And we shall rejoin: Yes; but our friend Gorgias contends that his art produces a greater good than yours. And then he will be sure to go on and ask, "What good? Let Gorgias answer." Now I want you, Gorgias, to imagine that this question is asked of you by them and by me; What is that which, as you say, is the greatest good of man, and of which you are the creator? Answer us.

GORGIAS: That good, Socrates, which is truly the greatest, being that which gives to men freedom in their own persons, and to individuals the power of ruling over others in their several states.

SOCRATES: And what would you consider this to be?

GORGIAS: What is there greater than the word which persuades the judges in the courts, or the senators in the council, or the citizens in the assembly, or at any other political meeting?–if you have the power of uttering this word, you will have the physician your slave, and the trainer your slave, and the money-maker of whom you talk will be found to gather treasures, not for himself, but for you who are able to speak and to persuade the multitude.

SOCRATES: Now I think, Gorgias, that you have very accurately explained what you conceive to be the art of rhetoric; and you mean to say, if I am not mistaken, that rhetoric is the artificer of persuasion, having this and no other business, and that this is her crown and end. Do you know any other effect of rhetoric over and above that of producing persuasion?

GORGIAS: No: the definition seems to me very fair, Socrates; for persuasion is the chief end of rhetoric.

SOCRATES: Then hear me, Gorgias, for I am quite sure that if there ever was a man who entered on the discussion of a matter from a pure love of knowing the truth, I am such a one, and I should say the same of you.

GORGIAS: What is coming, Socrates?

SOCRATES: I will tell you: I am very well aware that I do not know what, according to you, is the exact nature, or what are the topics of that persuasion of which you speak, and which is given by rhetoric; although I have a suspicion about both the one and the other. And I am going to ask–what is this power of persuasion which is given by rhetoric, and about what? But why, if I have a suspicion, do I ask instead of telling you? Not for your sake, but in order that the argument may proceed in such a manner as is most likely to set forth the truth. And I would have you observe, that I am right in asking this further question: If I asked, "What sort of a painter is Zeuxis?" and you said, "The painter of figures," should I not be right in asking, "What kind of figures, and where do you find them?"

GORGIAS: Certainly.

SOCRATES: And the reason for asking this second question would be, that there are other painters besides, who paint many other figures?

GORGIAS: True.

SOCRATES: But if there had been no one but Zeuxis who painted them, then you would have answered very well?

GORGIAS: Quite so.

SOCRATES: Now I want to know about rhetoric in the same way;–is rhetoric the only art which brings persuasion, or do other arts have the same effect? I mean to say–Does he who teaches anything persuade men of that which he teaches or not?

GORGIAS: He persuades, Socrates,–there can be no mistake about that.

SOCRATES: Again, if we take the arts of which we were just now speaking:–do not arithmetic and the arithmeticians teach us the properties of number?

GORGIAS: Certainly.

SOCRATES: And therefore persuade us of them?

GORGIAS: Yes.

SOCRATES: Then arithmetic as well as rhetoric is an artificer of persuasion?

GORGIAS: Clearly.

SOCRATES: And if any one asks us what sort of persuasion, and about what,–we shall answer, persuasion which teaches the quantity of odd and even; and we shall be able to show that all the other arts of which we were just now speaking are artificers of persuasion, and of what sort, and about what.

GORGIAS: Very true.

SOCRATES: Then rhetoric is not the only artificer of persuasion?

GORGIAS: True.

SOCRATES: Seeing, then, that not only rhetoric works by persuasion, but that other arts do the same, as in the case of the painter, a question has arisen which is a very fair one: Of what persuasion is rhetoric the artificer, and about what?–is not that a fair way of putting the question?

GORGIAS: I think so.

SOCRATES: Then, if you approve the question, Gorgias, what is the answer?

GORGIAS: I answer, Socrates, that rhetoric is the art of persuasion in courts of law and other assemblies, as I was just now saying, and about the just and unjust.

SOCRATES: And that, Gorgias, was what I was suspecting to be your notion; yet I would not have you wonder if by-and-by I am found repeating a seemingly plain question; for I ask not in order to confute you, but as I was saying that the argument may proceed consecutively, and that we may not get the habit of anticipating and suspecting the meaning of one another's words; I would have you develope your own views in your own way, whatever may be your hypothesis.

GORGIAS: I think that you are quite right, Socrates.

SOCRATES: Then let me raise another question; there is such a thing as "having learned"?

GORGIAS: Yes.

SOCRATES: And there is also "having believed"?

GORGIAS: Yes.

SOCRATES: And is the "having learned" the same as "having believed," and are learning and belief the same things?

GORGIAS: In my judgment, Socrates, they are not the same.

SOCRATES: And your judgment is right, as you may ascertain in this way:–If a person were to say to you, "Is there, Gorgias, a false belief as well as a true?"–you would reply, if I am not mistaken, that there is.

GORGIAS: Yes.

SOCRATES: Well, but is there a false knowledge as well as a true?

GORGIAS: No.

SOCRATES: No, indeed; and this again proves that knowledge and belief differ.

GORGIAS: Very true.

SOCRATES: And yet those who have learned as well as those who have believed are persuaded?

GORGIAS: Just so.

SOCRATES: Shall we then assume two sorts of persuasion,–one which is the source of belief without knowledge, as the other is of knowledge?

GORGIAS: By all means.

SOCRATES: And which sort of persuasion does rhetoric create in courts of law and other assemblies about the just and unjust, the sort of persuasion which gives belief without knowledge, or that which gives knowledge?

GORGIAS: Clearly, Socrates, that which only gives belief.

SOCRATES: Then rhetoric, as would appear, is the artificer of a persuasion which creates belief about the just and unjust, but gives no instruction about them?

GORGIAS: True.

SOCRATES: And the rhetorician does not instruct the courts of law or other assemblies about things just and unjust, but he creates belief about them; for no one can be supposed to instruct such a vast multitude about such high matters in a short time?

GORGIAS: Certainly not.

SOCRATES: Come, then, and let us see what we really mean about rhetoric; for I do not know what my own meaning is as yet. When the assembly meets to elect a physician or a shipwright or any other craftsman, will the rhetorician be taken into counsel? Surely not. For at every election he ought to be chosen who is most skilled; and, again, when walls have to be built or harbours or docks to be constructed, not the rhetorician but the master workman will advise; or when generals have to be chosen and an order of battle arranged, or a position taken, then the military will advise and not the rhetoricians: what do you say, Gorgias? Since you profess to be a rhetorician and a maker of rhetoricians, I cannot do better than learn the nature of your art from you. And here let me assure you that I have your interest in view as well as my own. For likely enough some one or other of the young men present might desire to become your pupil, and in fact I see some, and a good many too, who have this wish, but they would be too modest to question you. And therefore when you are interrogated by me, I would have you imagine that you are interrogated by them. "What is the use of coming to you, Gorgias?" they will say–"about what will you teach us to advise the state?–about the just and unjust only, or about those other things also which Socrates has just mentioned?" How will you answer them?

GORGIAS: I like your way of leading us on, Socrates, and I will endeavour to reveal to you the whole nature of rhetoric. You must have heard, I think, that the docks and the walls of the Athenians and the plan of the harbour were devised in accordance with the counsels, partly of Themistocles, and partly of Pericles, and not at the suggestion of the builders.

SOCRATES: Such is the tradition, Gorgias, about Themistocles; and I myself heard the speech of Pericles when he advised us about the middle wall.

GORGIAS: And you will observe, Socrates, that when a decision has to be given in such matters the rhetoricians are the advisers; they are the men who win their point.

SOCRATES: I had that in my admiring mind, Gorgias, when I asked what is the nature of rhetoric, which always appears to me, when I look at the matter in this way, to be a marvel of greatness.

GORGIAS: A marvel, indeed, Socrates, if you only knew how rhetoric comprehends and holds under her sway all the inferior arts. Let me offer you a striking example of this. On several occasions I have been with my brother Herodicus or some other physician to see one of his patients, who would not allow the physician to give him medicine, or apply the knife or hot iron to him; and I have persuaded him to do for me what he would not do for the physician just by the use of rhetoric. And I say that if a rhetorician and a physician were to go to any city, and had there to argue in the Ecclesia or any other assembly as to which of them should be elected state-physician, the physician would have no chance; but he who could speak would be chosen if he wished; and in a contest with a man of any other profession the rhetorician more than any one would have the power of getting himself chosen, for he can speak more persuasively to the multitude than any of them, and on any subject. Such is the nature and power of the art of rhetoric! And yet, Socrates, rhetoric should be used like any other competitive art, not against everybody,–the rhetorician ought not to abuse his strength any more than a pugilist or pancratiast or other master of fence;–because he has powers which are more than a match either for friend or enemy, he ought not therefore to strike, stab, or slay his friends. Suppose a man to have been trained in the palestra and to be a skilful boxer,–he in the fulness of his strength goes and strikes his father or mother or one of his familiars or friends; but that is no reason why the trainers or fencing-masters should be held in detestation or banished from the city;–surely not. For they taught their art for a good purpose, to be used against enemies and evil-doers, in self-defence not in aggression, and others have perverted their instructions, and turned to a bad use their own strength and skill. But not on this account are the teachers bad, neither is the art in fault, or bad in itself; I should rather say that those who make a bad use of the art are to blame. And the same argument holds good of rhetoric; for the rhetorician can speak against all men and upon any subject,–in short, he can persuade the multitude better than any other man of anything which he pleases, but he should not therefore seek to defraud the physician or any other artist of his reputation merely because he has the power; he ought to use rhetoric fairly, as he would also use his athletic powers. And if after having become a rhetorician he makes a bad use of his strength and skill, his instructor surely ought not on that account to be held in detestation or banished. For he was intended by his teacher to make a good use of his instructions, but he abuses them. And therefore he is the person who ought to be held in detestation, banished, and put to death, and not his instructor.

SOCRATES: You, Gorgias, like myself, have had great experience of disputations, and you must have observed, I think, that they do not always terminate in mutual edification, or in the definition by either party of the subjects which they are discussing; but disagreements are apt to arise–somebody says that another has not spoken truly or clearly; and then they get into a passion and begin to quarrel, both parties conceiving that their opponents are arguing from personal feeling only and jealousy of themselves, not from any interest in the question at issue. And sometimes they will go on abusing one another until the company at last are quite vexed at themselves for ever listening to such fellows. Why do I say this? Why, because I cannot help feeling that you are now saying what is not quite consistent or accordant with what you were saying at first about rhetoric. And I am afraid to point this out to you, lest you should think that I have some animosity against you, and that I speak, not for the sake of discovering the truth, but from jealousy of you. Now if you are one of my sort, I should like to cross-examine you, but if not I will let you alone. And what is my sort? you will ask. I am one of those who are very willing to be refuted if I say anything which is not true, and very willing to refute any one else who says what is not true, and quite as ready to be refuted as to refute; for I hold that this is the greater gain of the two, just as the gain is greater of being cured of a very great evil than of curing another. For I imagine that there is no evil which a man can endure so great as an erroneous opinion about the matters of which we are speaking; and if you claim to be one of my sort, let us have the discussion out, but if you would rather have done, no matter;–let us make an end of it.

GORGIAS: I should say, Socrates, that I am quite the man whom you indicate; but, perhaps, we ought to consider the audience, for, before you came, I had already given a long exhibition, and if we proceed the argument may run on to a great length. And therefore I think that we should consider whether we may not be detaining some part of the company when they are wanting to do something else.

CHAEREPHON: You hear the audience cheering, Gorgias and Socrates, which shows their desire to listen to you; and for myself, Heaven forbid that I should have any business on hand which would take me away from a discussion so interesting and so ably maintained.

CALLICLES: By the gods, Chaerephon, although I have been present at many discussions, I doubt whether I was ever so much delighted before, and therefore if you go on discoursing all day I shall be the better pleased.

SOCRATES: I may truly say, Callicles, that I am willing, if Gorgias is.

GORGIAS: After all this, Socrates, I should be disgraced if I refused, especially as I have promised to answer all comers; in accordance with the wishes of the company, then, do you begin, and ask of me any question which you like.

SOCRATES: Let me tell you then, Gorgias, what surprises me in your words; though I dare say that you may be right, and I may have misunderstood your meaning. You say that you can make any man, who will learn of you, a rhetorician?

GORGIAS: Yes.

SOCRATES: Do you mean that you will teach him to gain the ears of the multitude on any subject, and this not by instruction but by persuasion?

GORGIAS: Quite so.

SOCRATES: You were saying, in fact, that the

rhetorician will have greater powers of persuasion than the physician even in a matter of health?

GORGIAS: Yes, with the multitude,–that is.

SOCRATES: You mean to say, with the ignorant; for with those who know he cannot be supposed to have greater powers of persuasion.

GORGIAS: Very true.

SOCRATES: But if he is to have more power of persuasion than the physician, he will have greater power than he who knows?

GORGIAS: Certainly.

SOCRATES: Although he is not a physician:–is he?

GORGIAS: No.

SOCRATES: And he who is not a physician must, obviously, be ignorant of what the physician knows.

GORGIAS: Clearly.

SOCRATES: Then, when the rhetorician is more persuasive than the physician, the ignorant is more persuasive with the ignorant than he who has knowledge?–is not that the inference?

GORGIAS: In the case supposed:–yes.

SOCRATES: And the same holds of the relation of rhetoric to all the other arts; the rhetorician need not know the truth about things; he has only to discover some way of persuading the ignorant that he has more knowledge than those who know?

GORGIAS: Yes, Socrates, and is not this a great comfort?–not to have learned the other arts, but the art of rhetoric only, and yet to be in no way inferior to the professors of them?

SOCRATES: Whether the rhetorician is or not inferior on this account is a question which we will hereafter examine if the enquiry is likely to be of any service to us; but I would rather begin by asking, whether he is or is not as ignorant of the just and unjust, base and honourable, good and evil, as he is of medicine and the other arts; I mean to say, does he really know anything of what is good and evil, base or honourable, just or unjust in them; or has he only a way with the ignorant of persuading them that he not knowing is to be esteemed to know more about these things than some one else who knows? Or must the pupil know these things and come to you knowing them before he can acquire the art of rhetoric? If he is ignorant, you who are the teacher of rhetoric will not teach him–it is not your business; but you will make him seem to the multitude to know them, when he does not know them; and seem to be a good man, when he is not. Or will you be unable to teach him rhetoric at all, unless he knows the truth of these things first? What is to be said about all this? By heavens, Gorgias, I wish that you would reveal to me the power of rhetoric, as you were saying that you would.

GORGIAS: Well, Socrates, I suppose that if the pupil does chance not to know them, he will have to learn of me these things as well.

SOCRATES: Say no more, for there you are right; and so he whom you make a rhetorician must either know the nature of the just and unjust already, or he must be taught by you.

GORGIAS: Certainly.

SOCRATES: Well, and is not he who has learned carpentering a carpenter?

GORGIAS: Yes.

SOCRATES: And he who has learned music a musician?

GORGIAS: Yes.

SOCRATES: And he who has learned medicine is a physician, in like manner? He who has learned anything whatever is that which his knowledge makes him.

GORGIAS: Certainly.

SOCRATES: And in the same way, he who has learned what is just is just?

GORGIAS: To be sure.

SOCRATES: And he who is just may be supposed to do what is just?

GORGIAS: Yes.

SOCRATES: And must not the just man always desire to do what is just?

GORGIAS: That is clearly the inference.

SOCRATES: Surely, then, the just man will never consent to do injustice?

GORGIAS: Certainly not.

SOCRATES: And according to the argument the rhetorician must be a just man?

GORGIAS: Yes.

SOCRATES: And will therefore never be willing to do injustice?

GORGIAS: Clearly not.

SOCRATES: But do you remember saying just now that the trainer is not to be accused or banished if the pugilist makes a wrong use of his pugilistic art; and in like manner, if the rhetorician makes a bad and unjust use of his rhetoric, that is not to be laid to the charge of his teacher, who is not to be banished, but the wrong-doer himself who made a bad use of his rhetoric–he is to be banished–was not that said?

GORGIAS: Yes, it was.

SOCRATES: But now we are affirming that the aforesaid rhetorician will never have done injustice at all?

GORGIAS: True.

SOCRATES: And at the very outset, Gorgias, it was said that rhetoric treated of discourse, not (like arithmetic) about odd and even, but about just and unjust? Was not this said?

GORGIAS: Yes.

SOCRATES: I was thinking at the time, when I heard you saying so, that rhetoric, which is always discoursing about justice, could not possibly be an unjust thing. But when you added, shortly afterwards, that the rhetorician might make a bad use of rhetoric I noted with surprise the inconsistency into which you had fallen; and I said, that if you thought, as I did, that there was a gain in being refuted, there would be an advantage in going on with the question, but if not, I would leave off. And in the course of our investigations, as you will see yourself, the rhetorician has been acknowledged to be incapable of making an unjust use of rhetoric, or of willingness to do injustice. By the dog, Gorgias, there will be a great deal of discussion, before we get at the truth of all this.

POLUS: And do even you, Socrates, seriously believe what you are now saying about rhetoric? What! because Gorgias was ashamed to deny that the rhetorician knew the just and the honourable and the good, and admitted that to any one who came to him ignorant of them he could teach them, and then out of this admission there arose a contradiction–the thing which you dearly love, and to which not he, but you, brought the argument by your captious questions–(do you seriously believe that there is any truth in all this?) For will any one ever acknowledge that he does not know, or cannot teach, the nature of justice? The truth is, that there is great want of manners in bringing the argument to such a pass.

SOCRATES: Illustrious Polus, the reason why we provide ourselves with friends and children is, that when we get old and stumble, a younger generation may be at hand to set us on our legs again in our words and in our actions: and now, if I and Gorgias are stumbling, here are you who should raise us up; and I for my part engage to retract any error into which you may think that I have fallen-upon one condition:

POLUS: What condition?

SOCRATES: That you contract, Polus, the prolixity of speech in which you indulged at first.

POLUS: What! do you mean that I may not use as many words as I please?

SOCRATES: Only to think, my friend, that having come on a visit to Athens, which is the most free-spoken state in Hellas, you when you got there, and you alone, should be deprived of the power of speech–that would be hard indeed. But then consider my case:–shall not I be very hardly used, if, when you are making a long oration, and refusing to answer what you are asked, I am compelled to stay and listen to you, and may not go away? I say rather, if you have a real interest in the argument, or, to repeat my former expression, have any desire to set it on its legs, take back any statement which you please; and in your turn ask and answer, like myself and Gorgias–refute and be refuted: for I suppose that you would claim to know what Gorgias knows–would you not?

POLUS: Yes.

SOCRATES: And you, like him, invite any one to ask you about anything which he pleases, and you will know how to answer him?

POLUS: To be sure.

SOCRATES: And now, which will you do, ask or answer?

POLUS: I will ask; and do you answer me, Socrates, the same question which Gorgias, as you suppose, is unable to answer: What is rhetoric?

SOCRATES: Do you mean what sort of an art?

POLUS: Yes.

SOCRATES: To say the truth, Polus, it is not an art at all, in my opinion.

POLUS: Then what, in your opinion, is rhetoric?

SOCRATES: A thing which, as I was lately reading in a book of yours, you say that you have made an art.

POLUS: What thing?

SOCRATES: I should say a sort of experience.

POLUS: Does rhetoric seem to you to be an experience?

SOCRATES: That is my view, but you may be of another mind.

POLUS: An experience in what?

SOCRATES: An experience in producing a sort of delight and gratification.

POLUS: And if able to gratify others, must not rhetoric be a fine thing?

SOCRATES: What are you saying, Polus? Why do you ask me whether rhetoric is a fine thing or not, when I have not as yet told you what rhetoric is?

POLUS: Did I not hear you say that rhetoric was a sort of experience?

SOCRATES: Will you, who are so desirous to gratify others, afford a slight gratification to me?

POLUS: I will.

SOCRATES: Will you ask me, what sort of an art is cookery?

POLUS: What sort of an art is cookery?

SOCRATES: Not an art at all, Polus.

POLUS: What then?

SOCRATES: I should say an experience.

POLUS: In what? I wish that you would explain to me.

SOCRATES: An experience in producing a sort of delight and gratification, Polus.

POLUS: Then are cookery and rhetoric the same?

SOCRATES: No, they are only different parts of the same profession.

POLUS: Of what profession?

SOCRATES: I am afraid that the truth may seem discourteous; and I hesitate to answer, lest Gorgias should imagine that I am making fun of his own profession. For whether or not this is that art of rhetoric which Gorgias practises I really cannot tell:–from what he was just now saying, nothing appeared of what he thought of his art, but the rhetoric which I mean is a part of a not very creditable whole.

GORGIAS: A part of what, Socrates? Say what you mean, and never mind me.

SOCRATES: In my opinion then, Gorgias, the whole of which rhetoric is a part is not an art at all, but the habit of a bold and ready wit, which knows how to manage mankind: this habit I sum up under the word "flattery"; and it appears to me to have many other parts, one of which is cookery, which may seem to be an art, but, as I maintain, is only an experience or routine and not an art:–another part is rhetoric, and the art of attiring and sophistry are two others: thus there are four branches, and four different things answering to them. And Polus may ask, if he likes, for he has not as yet been informed, what part of flattery is rhetoric: he did not see that I had not yet answered him when he proceeded to ask a further question: Whether I do not think rhetoric a fine thing? But I shall not tell him whether rhetoric is a fine thing or not, until I have first answered, "What is rhetoric?" For that would not be right, Polus; but I shall be happy to answer, if you will ask me, What part of flattery is rhetoric?

POLUS: I will ask and do you answer? What part of flattery is rhetoric?

SOCRATES: Will you understand my answer? Rhetoric, according to my view, is the ghost or counterfeit of a part of politics.

POLUS: And noble or ignoble?

SOCRATES: Ignoble, I should say, if I am compelled to answer, for I call what is bad ignoble: though I doubt whether you understand what I was saying before.

GORGIAS: Indeed, Socrates, I cannot say that I understand myself.

SOCRATES: I do not wonder, Gorgias; for I have not as yet explained myself, and our friend Polus, colt by name and colt by nature, is apt to run away. (This is an untranslatable play on the name "Polus," which means "a colt.")

GORGIAS: Never mind him, but explain to me what you mean by saying that rhetoric is the counterfeit of a part of politics.

SOCRATES: I will try, then, to explain my notion of rhetoric, and if I am mistaken, my friend Polus shall refute me. We may assume the existence of bodies and of souls?

GORGIAS: Of course.

SOCRATES: You would further admit that there is a good condition of either of them?

GORGIAS: Yes.

SOCRATES: Which condition may not be really good, but good only in appearance? I mean to say, that there are many persons who appear to be in good health, and whom only a physician or trainer will discern at first sight not to be in good health.

GORGIAS: True.

SOCRATES: And this applies not only to the body, but also to the soul: in either there may be that which gives the appearance of health and not the reality?

GORGIAS: Yes, certainly.

SOCRATES: And now I will endeavour to explain to you more clearly what I mean: The soul and body being two, have two arts corresponding to them: there is the art of politics attending on the soul; and another art attending on the body, of which I know no single name, but which may be described as having two divisions, one of them gymnastic, and the other medicine. And in politics there is a legislative part, which answers to gymnastic, as justice does to medicine; and the two parts run into one another, justice having to do with the same subject as legislation, and medicine with the same subject as gymnastic, but with a difference. Now, seeing that there are these four arts, two attending on the body and two on the soul for their highest good; flattery knowing, or rather guessing their natures, has distributed herself into four shams or simulations of them; she puts on the likeness of some one or other of them, and pretends to be that which she simulates, and having no regard for men's highest interests, is ever making pleasure the bait of the unwary, and deceiving them into the belief that she is of the highest value to them. Cookery simulates the disguise of medicine, and pretends to know what food is the best for the body; and if the physician and the cook had to enter into a competition in which children were the judges, or men who had no more sense than children, as to which of them best understands the goodness or badness of food, the physician would be starved to death. A flattery I deem this to be and of an ignoble sort, Polus, for to you I am now addressing myself, because it aims at pleasure without any thought of the best. An art I do not call it, but only an experience, because it is unable to explain or to give a reason of the nature of its own applications. And I do not call any irrational thing an art; but if you dispute my words, I am prepared to argue in defence of them.

Cookery, then, I maintain to be a flattery which takes the form of medicine; and tiring, in like manner, is a flattery which takes the form of gymnastic, and is knavish, false, ignoble, illiberal, working deceitfully by the help of lines, and colours, and enamels, and garments, and making men affect a spurious beauty to the neglect of the true beauty which is given by gymnastic.

I would rather not be tedious, and therefore I will only say, after the manner of the geometricians (for I think that by this time you will be able to follow)

as tiring: gymnastic:: cookery: medicine;
or rather,
as tiring: gymnastic:: sophistry: legislation;
and
as cookery: medicine:: rhetoric: justice.

And this, I say, is the natural difference between the rhetorician and the sophist, but by reason of their near connection, they are apt to be jumbled up together; neither do they know what to make of themselves, nor do other men know what to make of them. For if the body presided over itself, and were not under the guidance of the soul, and the soul did not discern and discriminate between cookery and medicine, but the body was made the judge of them, and the rule of judgment was the bodily delight which was given by them, then the word of Anaxagoras, that word with which you, friend Polus, are so well acquainted, would prevail far and wide: "Chaos" would come again, and cookery, health, and medicine would mingle in an indiscriminate mass. And now I have told you my notion of rhetoric, which is, in relation to the soul, what cookery is to the body. I may have been inconsistent in making a long speech, when I would not allow you to discourse at length. But I think that I may be excused, because you did not understand me, and could make no use of my answer when I spoke shortly, and therefore I had to enter into an explanation. And if I show an equal inability to make use of yours, I hope that you will speak at equal length; but if I am able to understand you, let me have the benefit of your brevity, as is only fair: And now you may do what you please with my answer.

POLUS: What do you mean? do you think that rhetoric is flattery?

SOCRATES: Nay, I said a part of flattery; if at your age, Polus, you cannot remember, what will you do by-and-by, when you get older?

POLUS: And are the good rhetoricians meanly regarded in states, under the idea that they are flatterers?

SOCRATES: Is that a question or the beginning of a speech?

POLUS: I am asking a question.

SOCRATES: Then my answer is, that they are not regarded at all.

POLUS: How not regarded? Have they not very great power in states?

SOCRATES: Not if you mean to say that power is a good to the possessor.

POLUS: And that is what I do mean to say.

SOCRATES: Then, if so, I think that they have the least power of all the citizens.

POLUS: What! are they not like tyrants? They kill and despoil and exile any one whom they please.

SOCRATES: By the dog, Polus, I cannot make out at each deliverance of yours, whether you are giving an opinion of your own, or asking a question of me.

POLUS: I am asking a question of you.

SOCRATES: Yes, my friend, but you ask two questions at once.

POLUS: How two questions?

SOCRATES: Why, did you not say just now that the rhetoricians are like tyrants, and that they kill and despoil or exile any one whom they please?

POLUS: I did.

SOCRATES: Well then, I say to you that here are two questions in one, and I will answer both of them. And I tell you, Polus, that rhetoricians and tyrants have the least possible power in states, as I was just now saying; for they do literally nothing which they will, but only what they think best.

POLUS: And is not that a great power?

SOCRATES: Polus has already said the reverse.

POLUS: Said the reverse! nay, that is what I assert.

SOCRATES: No, by the great–what do you call him?–not you, for you say that power is a good to him who has the power.

POLUS: I do.

SOCRATES: And would you maintain that if a fool does what he thinks best, this is a good, and would you call this great power?

POLUS: I should not.

SOCRATES: Then you must prove that the rhetorician is not a fool, and that rhetoric is an art and not a flattery–and so you will have refuted me; but if you leave me unrefuted, why, the rhetoricians who do what they think best in states, and the tyrants, will have nothing upon which to congratulate themselves, if as you say, power be indeed a good, admitting at the same time that what is done without sense is an evil.

POLUS: Yes; I admit that.

SOCRATES: How then can the rhetoricians or the tyrants have great power in states, unless Polus can refute Socrates, and prove to him that they do as they will?

POLUS: This fellow–

SOCRATES: I say that they do not do as they will;–now refute me.

POLUS: Why, have you not already said that they do as they think best?

SOCRATES: And I say so still.

POLUS: Then surely they do as they will?

SOCRATES: I deny it.

POLUS: But they do what they think best?

SOCRATES: Aye.

POLUS: That, Socrates, is monstrous and absurd.

SOCRATES: Good words, good Polus, as I may say in your own peculiar style; but if you have any questions to ask of me, either prove that I am in error or give the answer yourself.

POLUS: Very well, I am willing to answer that I may know what you mean.

SOCRATES: Do men appear to you to will that which they do, or to will that further end for the sake of which they do a thing? when they take medicine, for example, at the bidding of a physician, do they will the drinking of the medicine which is painful, or the health for the sake of which they drink?

POLUS: Clearly, the health.

SOCRATES: And when men go on a voyage or engage in business, they do not will that which they are doing at the time; for who would desire to take the risk of a voyage or the trouble of business?–But they will, to have the wealth for the sake of which they go on a voyage.

POLUS: Certainly.

SOCRATES: And is not this universally true? If a man does something for the sake of something else, he wills not that which he does, but that for the sake of which he does it.

POLUS: Yes.

SOCRATES: And are not all things either good or evil, or intermediate and indifferent?

POLUS: To be sure, Socrates.

SOCRATES: Wisdom and health and wealth and the like you would call goods, and their opposites evils?

POLUS: I should.

SOCRATES: And the things which are neither good nor evil, and which partake sometimes of the nature of good and at other times of evil, or of neither, are such as sitting, walking, running, sailing; or, again, wood, stones, and the like:–these are the things which you call neither good nor evil?

POLUS: Exactly so.

SOCRATES: Are these indifferent things done for the sake of the good, or the good for the sake of the indifferent?

POLUS: Clearly, the indifferent for the sake of the good.

SOCRATES: When we walk we walk for the sake of the good, and under the idea that it is better to walk, and when we stand we stand equally for the sake of the good?

POLUS: Yes.

SOCRATES: And when we kill a man we kill him or exile him or despoil him of his goods, because, as we think, it will conduce to our good?

POLUS: Certainly.

SOCRATES: Men who do any of these things do them for the sake of the good?

POLUS: Yes.

SOCRATES: And did we not admit that in doing something for the sake of something else, we do not will those things which we do, but that other thing for the sake of which we do them?

POLUS: Most true.

SOCRATES: Then we do not will simply to kill a man or to exile him or to despoil him of his goods, but we will to do that which conduces to our good, and if the act is not conducive to our good we do not will it; for we will, as you say, that which is our good, but that which is neither good nor evil, or simply evil, we do not will. Why are you silent, Polus? Am I not right?

POLUS: You are right.

SOCRATES: Hence we may infer, that if any one, whether he be a tyrant or a rhetorician, kills another or exiles another or deprives him of his property, under the idea that the act is for his own interests when really not for his own interests, he may be said to do what seems best to him?

POLUS: Yes.

SOCRATES: But does he do what he wills if he does what is evil? Why do you not answer?

POLUS: Well, I suppose not.

SOCRATES: Then if great power is a good as you allow, will such a one have great power in a state?

POLUS: He will not.

SOCRATES: Then I was right in saying that a man may do what seems good to him in a state, and not have great power, and not do what he wills?

POLUS: As though you, Socrates, would not like to have the power of doing what seemed good to you in the state, rather than not; you would not be jealous when you saw any one killing or despoiling or imprisoning whom he pleased, Oh, no!

SOCRATES: Justly or unjustly, do you mean?

POLUS: In either case is he not equally to be envied?

SOCRATES: Forbear, Polus!

POLUS: Why "forbear"?

SOCRATES: Because you ought not to envy wretches who are not to be envied, but only to pity them.

POLUS: And are those of whom I spoke wretches?

SOCRATES: Yes, certainly they are.

POLUS: And so you think that he who slays any one whom he pleases, and justly slays him, is pitiable and wretched?

SOCRATES: No, I do not say that of him: but neither do I think that he is to be envied.

POLUS: Were you not saying just now that he is wretched?

SOCRATES: Yes, my friend, if he killed another unjustly, in which case he is also to be pitied; and he is not to be envied if he killed him justly.

POLUS: At any rate you will allow that he who is unjustly put to death is wretched, and to be pitied?

SOCRATES: Not so much, Polus, as he who kills him, and not so much as he who is justly killed.

POLUS: How can that be, Socrates?

SOCRATES: That may very well be, inasmuch as doing injustice is the greatest of evils.

POLUS: But is it the greatest? Is not suffering injustice a greater evil?

SOCRATES: Certainly not.

POLUS: Then would you rather suffer than do injustice?

SOCRATES: I should not like either, but if I must choose between them, I would rather suffer than do.

POLUS: Then you would not wish to be a tyrant?

SOCRATES: Not if you mean by tyranny what I mean.

POLUS: I mean, as I said before, the power of doing whatever seems good to you in a state, killing, banishing, doing in all things as you like.

SOCRATES: Well then, illustrious friend, when I have said my say, do you reply to me. Suppose that I go into a crowded Agora, and take a dagger under my arm. Polus, I say to you, I have just acquired rare power, and become a tyrant; for if I think that any of these men whom you see ought to be put to death, the man whom I have a mind to kill is as good as dead; and if I am disposed to break his head or tear his garment, he will have his head broken or his garment torn in an instant. Such is my great power in this city. And if you do not believe me, and I show you the dagger, you would probably reply: Socrates, in that sort of way any one may have great power–he may burn any house which he pleases, and the docks and triremes of the Athenians, and all their other vessels, whether public or private–but can you believe that this mere doing as you think best is great power?

POLUS: Certainly not such doing as this.

SOCRATES: But can you tell me why you disapprove of such a power?

POLUS: I can.

SOCRATES: Why then?

POLUS: Why, because he who did as you say would be certain to be punished.

SOCRATES: And punishment is an evil?

POLUS: Certainly.

SOCRATES: And you would admit once more, my good sir, that great power is a benefit to a man if his actions turn out to his advantage, and that this is the meaning of great power; and if not, then his power is an evil and is no power. But let us look at the matter in another way:–do we not acknowledge that the things of which we were speaking, the infliction of death, and exile, and the deprivation of property are sometimes a good and sometimes not a good?

POLUS: Certainly.

SOCRATES: About that you and I may be supposed to agree?

POLUS: Yes.

SOCRATES: Tell me, then, when do you say that they are good and when that they are evil–what principle do you lay down?

POLUS: I would rather, Socrates, that you should answer as well as ask that question.

SOCRATES: Well, Polus, since you would rather have the answer from me, I say that they are good when they are just, and evil when they are unjust.

POLUS: You are hard of refutation, Socrates, but might not a child refute that statement?

SOCRATES: Then I shall be very grateful to the child, and equally grateful to you if you will refute me and deliver me from my foolishness. And I hope that refute me you will, and not weary of doing good to a friend.

POLUS: Yes, Socrates, and I need not go far or appeal to antiquity; events which happened only a few days ago are enough to refute you, and to prove that many men who do wrong are happy.

SOCRATES: What events?

POLUS: You see, I presume, that Archelaus the son of Perdiccas is now the ruler of Macedonia?

SOCRATES: At any rate I hear that he is.

POLUS: And do you think that he is happy or miserable?

SOCRATES: I cannot say, Polus, for I have never had any acquaintance with him.

POLUS: And cannot you tell at once, and without having an acquaintance with him, whether a man is happy?

SOCRATES: Most certainly not.

POLUS: Then clearly, Socrates, you would say that you did not even know whether the great king was a happy man?

SOCRATES: And I should speak the truth; for I do not know how he stands in the matter of education and justice.

POLUS: What! and does all happiness consist in this?

SOCRATES: Yes, indeed, Polus, that is my doctrine; the men and women who are gentle and good are also happy, as I maintain, and the unjust and evil are miserable.

POLUS: Then, according to your doctrine, the said Archelaus is miserable?

SOCRATES: Yes, my friend, if he is wicked.

POLUS: That he is wicked I cannot deny; for he had no title at all to the throne which he now occupies, he being only the son of a woman who was the slave of Alcetas the brother of Perdiccas; he himself therefore in strict right was the slave of Alcetas; and if he had meant to do rightly he would have remained his slave, and then, according to your doctrine, he would have been happy. But now he is unspeakably miserable, for he has been guilty of the greatest crimes: in the first place he invited his uncle and master, Alcetas, to come to him, under the pretence that he would restore to him the throne which Perdiccas has usurped, and after entertaining him and his son Alexander, who was his own cousin, and nearly of an age with him, and making them drunk, he threw them into a waggon and carried them off by night, and slew them, and got both of them out of the way; and when he had done all this wickedness he never discovered that he was the most miserable of all men, and was very far from repenting: shall I tell you how he showed his remorse? he had a younger brother, a child of seven years old, who was the legitimate son of Perdiccas, and to him of right the kingdom belonged; Archelaus, however, had no mind to bring him up as he ought and restore the kingdom to him; that was not his notion of happiness; but not long afterwards he threw him into a well and drowned him, and declared to his mother Cleopatra that he had fallen in while running after a goose, and had been killed. And now as he is the greatest criminal of all the Macedonians, he may be supposed to be the most miserable and not the happiest of them, and I dare say that there are many Athenians, and you would be at the head of them, who would rather be any other Macedonian than Archelaus!

SOCRATES: I praised you at first, Polus, for being a rhetorician rather than a reasoner. And this, as I suppose, is the sort of argument with which you fancy that a child might refute me, and by which I stand refuted when I say that the unjust man is not happy. But, my good friend, where is the refutation? I cannot admit a word which you have been saying.

POLUS: That is because you will not; for you surely must think as I do.

SOCRATES: Not so, my simple friend, but because you will refute me after the manner which rhetoricians practise in courts of law. For there the one party think that they refute the other when they bring forward a number of witnesses of good repute in proof of their allegations, and their adversary has only a single one or none at all. But this kind of proof is of no value where truth is the aim; a man may often be sworn down by a multitude of false witnesses who have a great air of respectability. And in this argument nearly every one, Athenian and stranger alike, would be on your side, if you should bring witnesses in disproof of my statement;–you may, if you will, summon Nicias the son of Niceratus, and let his brothers, who gave the row of tripods which stand in the precincts of Dionysus, come with him; or you may summon Aristocrates, the son of Scellius, who is the giver of that famous offering which is at Delphi; summon, if you will, the whole house of Pericles, or any other great Athenian family whom you choose;–they will all agree with you: I only am left alone and cannot agree, for you do not convince me; although you produce many false witnesses against me, in the hope of depriving me of my inheritance, which is the truth. But I consider that nothing worth speaking of will have been effected by me unless I make you the one witness of my words; nor by you, unless you make me the one witness of yours; no matter about the rest of the world. For there are two ways of refutation, one which is yours and that of the world in general; but mine is of another sort–let us compare them, and see in what they differ. For, indeed, we are at issue about matters which to know is honourable and not to know disgraceful; to know or not to know happiness and misery–that is the chief of them. And what knowledge can be nobler? or what ignorance more disgraceful than this? And therefore I will begin by asking you whether you do not think that a man who is unjust and doing injustice can be happy, seeing that you think Archelaus unjust, and yet happy? May I assume this to be your opinion?

POLUS: Certainly.

SOCRATES: But I say that this is an impossibility–here is one point about which we are at issue:–very good. And do you mean to say also that if he meets with retribution and punishment he will still be happy?

POLUS: Certainly not; in that case he will be most miserable.

SOCRATES: On the other hand, if the unjust be not punished, then, according to you, he will be happy?

POLUS: Yes.

SOCRATES: But in my opinion, Polus, the unjust or doer of unjust actions is miserable in any case,–more miserable, however, if he be not punished and does not meet with retribution, and less miserable if he be punished and meets with retribution at the hands of gods and men.

POLUS: You are maintaining a strange doctrine, Socrates.

SOCRATES: I shall try to make you agree with me, O my friend, for as a friend I regard you. Then these are the points at issue between us–are they not? I was saying that to do is worse than to suffer injustice?

POLUS: Exactly so.

SOCRATES: And you said the opposite?

POLUS: Yes.

SOCRATES: I said also that the wicked are miserable, and you refuted me?

POLUS: By Zeus, I did.

SOCRATES: In your own opinion, Polus.

POLUS: Yes, and I rather suspect that I was in the right.

SOCRATES: You further said that the wrong-doer is happy if he be unpunished?

POLUS: Certainly.

SOCRATES: And I affirm that he is most miserable, and that those who are punished are less miserable–are you going to refute this proposition also?

POLUS: A proposition which is harder of refutation than the other, Socrates.

SOCRATES: Say rather, Polus, impossible; for who can refute the truth?

POLUS: What do you mean? If a man is detected in an unjust attempt to make himself a tyrant, and when detected is racked, mutilated, has his eyes burned out, and after having had all sorts of great injuries inflicted on him, and having seen his wife and children suffer the like, is at last impaled or tarred and burned alive, will he be happier than if he escape and become a tyrant, and continue all through life doing what he likes and holding the reins of government, the envy and admiration both of citizens and strangers? Is that the paradox which, as you say, cannot be refuted?

SOCRATES: There again, noble Polus, you are raising hobgoblins instead of refuting me; just now you were calling witnesses against me. But please to refresh my memory a little; did you say–"xin an unjust attempt to make himself a tyrant"?

POLUS: Yes, I did.

SOCRATES: Then I say that neither of them will be happier than the other,–neither he who unjustly acquires a tyranny, nor he who suffers in the attempt, for of two miserables one cannot be the happier, but that he who escapes and becomes a tyrant is the more miserable of the two. Do you laugh, Polus? Well, this is a new kind of refutation,–when any one says anything, instead of refuting him to laugh at him.

POLUS: But do you not think, Socrates, that you have been sufficiently refuted, when you say that which no human being will allow? Ask the company.

SOCRATES: O Polus, I am not a public man, and only last year, when my tribe were serving as Prytanes, and it became my duty as their president to take the votes, there was a laugh at me, because I was unable to take them. And as I failed then, you must not ask me to count the suffrages of the company now; but if, as I was saying, you have no better argument than numbers, let me have a turn, and do you make trial of the sort of proof which, as I think, is required; for I shall produce one witness only of the truth of my words, and he is the person with whom I am arguing; his suffrage I know how to take; but with the many I have nothing to do, and do not even address myself to them. May I ask then whether you will answer in turn and have your words put to the proof? For I certainly think that I and you and every man do really believe, that to do is a greater evil than to suffer injustice: and not to be punished than to be punished.

POLUS: And I should say neither I, nor any man: would you yourself, for example, suffer rather than do injustice?

SOCRATES: Yes, and you, too; I or any man would.

POLUS: Quite the reverse; neither you, nor I, nor any man.

SOCRATES: But will you answer?

POLUS: To be sure, I will; for I am curious to hear what you can have to say.

SOCRATES: Tell me, then, and you will know, and let us suppose that I am beginning at the beginning: which of the two, Polus, in your opinion, is the worst?–to do injustice or to suffer?

POLUS: I should say that suffering was worst.

SOCRATES: And which is the greater disgrace?—Answer.

POLUS: To do.

SOCRATES: And the greater disgrace is the greater evil?

POLUS: Certainly not.

SOCRATES: I understand you to say, if I am not mistaken, that the honourable is not the same as the good, or the disgraceful as the evil?

POLUS: Certainly not.

SOCRATES: Let me ask a question of you: When you speak of beautiful things, such as bodies, colours, figures, sounds, institutions, do you not call them beautiful in reference to some standard: bodies, for example, are beautiful in proportion as they are useful, or as the sight of them gives pleasure to the spectators; can you give any other account of personal beauty?

POLUS: I cannot.

SOCRATES: And you would say of figures or colours generally that they were beautiful, either by reason of the pleasure which they give, or of their use, or of both?

POLUS: Yes, I should.

SOCRATES: And you would call sounds and music beautiful for the same reason?

POLUS: I should.

SOCRATES: Laws and institutions also have no beauty in them except in so far as they are useful or pleasant or both?

POLUS: I think not.

SOCRATES: And may not the same be said of the beauty of knowledge?

POLUS: To be sure, Socrates; and I very much approve of your measuring beauty by the standard of pleasure and utility.

SOCRATES: And deformity or disgrace may be equally measured by the opposite standard of pain and evil?

POLUS: Certainly.

SOCRATES: Then when of two beautiful things one exceeds in beauty, the measure of the excess is to be taken in one or both of these; that is to say, in pleasure or utility or both?

POLUS: Very true.

SOCRATES: And of two deformed things, that which exceeds in deformity or disgrace, exceeds either in pain or evil–must it not be so?

POLUS: Yes.

SOCRATES: But then again, what was the observation which you just now made, about doing and suffering wrong? Did you not say, that suffering wrong was more evil, and doing wrong more disgraceful?

POLUS: I did.

SOCRATES: Then, if doing wrong is more disgraceful than suffering, the more disgraceful must be more painful and must exceed in pain or in evil or both: does not that also follow?

POLUS: Of course.

SOCRATES: First, then, let us consider whether the doing of injustice exceeds the suffering in the consequent pain: Do the injurers suffer more than the injured?

POLUS: No, Socrates; certainly not.

SOCRATES: Then they do not exceed in pain?

POLUS: No.

SOCRATES: But if not in pain, then not in both?

POLUS: Certainly not.

SOCRATES: Then they can only exceed in the other?

POLUS: Yes.

SOCRATES: That is to say, in evil?

POLUS: True.

SOCRATES: Then doing injustice will have an excess of evil, and will therefore be a greater evil than suffering injustice?

POLUS: Clearly.

SOCRATES: But have not you and the world already agreed that to do injustice is more disgraceful than to suffer?

POLUS: Yes.

SOCRATES: And that is now discovered to be more evil?

POLUS: True.

SOCRATES: And would you prefer a greater evil or a greater dishonour to a less one? Answer, Polus, and fear not; for you will come to no harm if you nobly resign yourself into the healing hand of the argument as to a physician without shrinking, and either say "Yes" or "No" to me.

POLUS: I should say "No."

SOCRATES: Would any other man prefer a greater to a less evil?

POLUS: No, not according to this way of putting the case, Socrates.

SOCRATES: Then I said truly, Polus, that neither you, nor I, nor any man, would rather do than suffer injustice; for to do injustice is the greater evil of the two.

POLUS: That is the conclusion.

SOCRATES: You see, Polus, when you compare the two kinds of refutations, how unlike they are. All men, with the exception of myself, are of your way of thinking; but your single assent and witness are enough for me,–I have no need of any other, I take your suffrage, and am regardless of the rest. Enough of this, and now let us proceed to the next question; which is, Whether the greatest of evils to a guilty man is to suffer punishment, as you supposed, or whether to escape punishment is not a greater evil, as I supposed. Consider:–You would say that to suffer punishment is another name for being justly corrected when you do wrong?

POLUS: I should.

SOCRATES: And would you not allow that all just things are honourable in so far as they are just? Please to reflect, and tell me your opinion.

POLUS: Yes, Socrates, I think that they are.

SOCRATES: Consider again:–Where there is an agent, must there not also be a patient?

POLUS: I should say so.

SOCRATES: And will not the patient suffer that which the agent does, and will not the suffering have the quality of the action? I mean, for example, that if a man strikes, there must be something which is stricken?

POLUS: Yes.

SOCRATES: And if the striker strikes violently or quickly, that which is struck will be struck violently or quickly?

POLUS: True.

SOCRATES: And the suffering to him who is stricken is of the same nature as the act of him who strikes?

POLUS: Yes.

SOCRATES: And if a man burns, there is something which is burned?

POLUS: Certainly.

SOCRATES: And if he burns in excess or so as to cause pain, the thing burned will be burned in the same way?

POLUS: Truly.

SOCRATES: And if he cuts, the same argument holds–there will be something cut?

POLUS: Yes.

SOCRATES: And if the cutting be great or deep or such as will cause pain, the cut will be of the same nature?

POLUS: That is evident.

SOCRATES: Then you would agree generally to the universal proposition which I was just now asserting: that the affection of the patient answers to the affection of the agent?

POLUS: I agree.

SOCRATES: Then, as this is admitted, let me ask whether being punished is suffering or acting?

POLUS: Suffering, Socrates; there can be no doubt of that.

SOCRATES: And suffering implies an agent?

POLUS: Certainly, Socrates; and he is the punisher.

SOCRATES: And he who punishes rightly, punishes justly?

POLUS: Yes.

SOCRATES: And therefore he acts justly?

POLUS: Justly.

SOCRATES: Then he who is punished and suffers retribution, suffers justly?

POLUS: That is evident.

SOCRATES: And that which is just has been admitted to be honourable?

POLUS: Certainly.

SOCRATES: Then the punisher does what is honourable, and the punished suffers what is honourable?

POLUS: True.

SOCRATES: And if what is honourable, then what is good, for the honourable is either pleasant or useful?

POLUS: Certainly.

SOCRATES: Then he who is punished suffers what is good?

POLUS: That is true.

SOCRATES: Then he is benefited?

POLUS: Yes.

SOCRATES: Do I understand you to mean what I mean by the term "benefited"? I mean, that if he be justly punished his soul is improved.

POLUS: Surely.

SOCRATES: Then he who is punished is delivered from the evil of his soul?

POLUS: Yes.

SOCRATES: And is he not then delivered from the greatest evil? Look at the matter in this way:–In respect of a man's estate, do you see any greater evil than poverty?

POLUS: There is no greater evil.

SOCRATES: Again, in a man's bodily frame, you would say that the evil is weakness and disease and deformity?

POLUS: I should.

SOCRATES: And do you not imagine that the soul likewise has some evil of her own?

POLUS: Of course.

SOCRATES: And this you would call injustice and ignorance and cowardice, and the like?

POLUS: Certainly.

SOCRATES: So then, in mind, body, and estate, which are three, you have pointed out three corresponding evils–injustice, disease, poverty?

POLUS: True.

SOCRATES: And which of the evils is the most disgraceful?–Is not the most disgraceful of them injustice, and in general the evil of the soul?

POLUS: By far the most.

SOCRATES: And if the most disgraceful, then also the worst?

POLUS: What do you mean, Socrates?

SOCRATES: I mean to say, that is most disgraceful has been already admitted to be most painful or hurtful, or both.

POLUS: Certainly.

SOCRATES: And now injustice and all evil in the soul has been admitted by us to be most disgraceful?

POLUS: It has been admitted.

SOCRATES: And most disgraceful either because most painful and causing excessive pain, or most hurtful, or both?

POLUS: Certainly.

SOCRATES: And therefore to be unjust and intemperate, and cowardly and ignorant, is more painful than to be poor and sick?

POLUS: Nay, Socrates; the painfulness does not appear to me to follow from your premises.

SOCRATES: Then, if, as you would argue, not more painful, the evil of the soul is of all evils the most disgraceful; and the excess of disgrace must be caused by some preternatural greatness, or extraordinary hurtfulness of the evil.

POLUS: Clearly.

SOCRATES: And that which exceeds most in hurtfulness will be the greatest of evils?

POLUS: Yes.

SOCRATES: Then injustice and intemperance, and in general the depravity of the soul, are the greatest of evils?

POLUS: That is evident.

SOCRATES: Now, what art is there which delivers us from poverty? Does not the art of making money?

POLUS: Yes.

SOCRATES: And what art frees us from disease? Does not the art of medicine?

POLUS: Very true.

SOCRATES: And what from vice and injustice? If you are not able to answer at once, ask yourself whither we go with the sick, and to whom we take them.

POLUS: To the physicians, Socrates.

SOCRATES: And to whom do we go with the unjust and intemperate?

POLUS: To the judges, you mean.

SOCRATES: –Who are to punish them?

POLUS: Yes.

SOCRATES: And do not those who rightly punish others, punish them in accordance with a certain rule of justice?

POLUS: Clearly.

SOCRATES: Then the art of money-making frees a man from poverty; medicine from disease; and justice from intemperance and injustice?

POLUS: That is evident.

SOCRATES: Which, then, is the best of these three?

POLUS: Will you enumerate them?

SOCRATES: Money-making, medicine, and justice.

POLUS: Justice, Socrates, far excels the two others.

SOCRATES: And justice, if the best, gives the greatest pleasure or advantage or both?

POLUS: Yes.

SOCRATES: But is the being healed a pleasant thing, and are those who are being healed pleased?

POLUS: I think not.

SOCRATES: A useful thing, then?

POLUS: Yes.

SOCRATES: Yes, because the patient is delivered from a great evil; and this is the advantage of enduring the pain–that you get well?

POLUS: Certainly.

SOCRATES: And would he be the happier man in his bodily condition, who is healed, or who never was out of health?

POLUS: Clearly he who was never out of health.

SOCRATES: Yes; for happiness surely does not consist in being delivered from evils, but in never having had them.

POLUS: True.

SOCRATES: And suppose the case of two persons who have some evil in their bodies, and that one of them is healed and delivered from evil, and another is not healed, but retains the evil–which of them is the most miserable?

POLUS: Clearly he who is not healed.

SOCRATES: And was not punishment said by us to be a deliverance from the greatest of evils, which is vice?

POLUS: True.

SOCRATES: And justice punishes us, and makes us more just, and is the medicine of our vice?

POLUS: True.

SOCRATES: He, then, has the first place in the scale of happiness who has never had vice in his soul; for this has been shown to be the greatest of evils.

POLUS: Clearly.

SOCRATES: And he has the second place, who is delivered from vice?

POLUS: True.

SOCRATES: That is to say, he who receives admonition and rebuke and punishment?

POLUS: Yes.

SOCRATES: Then he lives worst, who, having been unjust, has no deliverance from injustice?

POLUS: Certainly.

SOCRATES: That is, he lives worst who commits the greatest crimes, and who, being the most unjust of men, succeeds in escaping rebuke or correction or punishment; and this, as you say, has been accomplished by Archelaus and other tyrants and rhetoricians and potentates? (Compare Republic.)

POLUS: True.

SOCRATES: May not their way of proceeding, my friend, be compared to the conduct of a person who is afflicted with the worst of diseases and yet contrives not to pay the penalty to the physician for his sins against his constitution, and will not be cured, because, like a child, he is afraid of the pain of being burned or cut:–Is not that a parallel case?

POLUS: Yes, truly.

SOCRATES: He would seem as if he did not know the nature of health and bodily vigour; and if we are right, Polus, in our previous conclusions, they are in a like case who strive to evade justice, which they see to be painful, but are blind to the advantage which ensues from it, not knowing how far more miserable a companion a diseased soul is than a diseased body; a soul, I say, which is corrupt and unrighteous and unholy. And hence they do all that they can to avoid punishment and to avoid being released from the greatest of evils; they provide themselves with money and friends, and cultivate to the utmost their powers of persuasion. But if we, Polus, are right, do you see what follows, or shall we draw out the consequences in form?

POLUS: If you please.

SOCRATES: Is it not a fact that injustice, and the doing of injustice, is the greatest of evils?

POLUS: That is quite clear.

SOCRATES: And further, that to suffer punishment is the way to be released from this evil?

POLUS: True.

SOCRATES: And not to suffer, is to perpetuate the evil?

POLUS: Yes.

SOCRATES: To do wrong, then, is second only in the scale of evils; but to do wrong and not to be punished, is first and greatest of all?

POLUS: That is true.

SOCRATES: Well, and was not this the point in dispute, my friend? You deemed Archelaus happy, because he was a very great criminal and unpunished: I, on the other hand, maintained that he or any other who like him has done wrong and has not been punished, is, and ought to be, the most miserable of all men; and that the doer of injustice is more miserable than the sufferer; and he who escapes punishment, more miserable than he who suffers.–Was not that what I said?

POLUS: Yes.

SOCRATES: And it has been proved to be true?

POLUS: Certainly.

SOCRATES: Well, Polus, but if this is true, where is the great use of rhetoric? If we admit what has been just now said, every man ought in every way to guard himself against doing wrong, for he will thereby suffer great evil?

POLUS: True.

SOCRATES: And if he, or any one about whom he cares, does wrong, he ought of his own accord to go where he will be immediately punished; he will run to the judge, as he would to the physician, in order that the disease of injustice may not be rendered chronic and become the incurable cancer of the soul; must we not allow this consequence, Polus, if our former admissions are to stand:–is any other inference consistent with them?

POLUS: To that, Socrates, there can be but one answer.

SOCRATES: Then rhetoric is of no use to us, Polus, in helping a man to excuse his own injustice, that of his parents or friends, or children or country; but may be of use to any one who holds that instead of excusing he ought to accuse–himself above all, and in the next degree his family or any of his friends who may be doing wrong; he should bring to light the iniquity and not conceal it, that so the wrong-doer may suffer and be made whole; and he should even force himself and others not to shrink, but with closed eyes like brave men to let the physician operate with knife or searing iron, not regarding the pain, in the hope of attaining the good and the honourable; let him who has done things worthy of stripes, allow himself to be scourged, if of bonds, to be bound, if of a fine, to be fined, if of exile, to be exiled, if of death, to die, himself being the first to accuse himself and his own relations, and using rhetoric to this end, that his and their unjust actions may be made manifest, and that they themselves may be delivered from injustice, which is the greatest evil. Then, Polus, rhetoric would indeed be useful. Do you say "Yes" or "No" to that?

POLUS: To me, Socrates, what you are saying appears very strange, though probably in agreement with your premises.

SOCRATES: Is not this the conclusion, if the premises are not disproven?

POLUS: Yes; it certainly is.

SOCRATES: And from the opposite point of view, if indeed it be our duty to harm another, whether an enemy or not–I except the case of self-defence–then I have to be upon my guard–but if my enemy injures a third person, then in every sort of way, by word as well as deed, I should try to prevent his being punished, or appearing before the judge; and if he appears, I should contrive that he should escape, and not suffer punishment: if he has stolen a sum of money, let him keep what he has stolen and spend it on him and his, regardless of religion and justice; and if he have done things worthy of death, let him not die, but rather be immortal in his wickedness; or, if this is not possible, let him at any rate be allowed to live as long as he can. For such purposes, Polus, rhetoric may be useful, but is of small if of any use to him who is not intending to commit injustice; at least, there was no such use discovered by us in the previous discussion.

CALLICLES: Tell me, Chaerephon, is Socrates in earnest, or is he joking?

CHAEREPHON: I should say, Callicles, that he is in most profound earnest; but you may well ask him.

CALLICLES: By the gods, and I will. Tell me, Socrates, are you in earnest, or only in jest? For if you are in earnest, and what you say is true, is not the whole of human life turned upside down; and are we not doing, as would appear, in everything the opposite of what we ought to be doing?

SOCRATES: O Callicles, if there were not some community of feelings among mankind, however varying in different persons–I mean to say, if every man's feelings were peculiar to himself and were not shared by the rest of his species–I do not see how we could ever communicate our impressions to one another. I make this remark because I perceive that you and I have a common feeling. For we are lovers both, and both of us have two loves apiece:–I am the lover of Alcibiades, the son of Cleinias, and of philosophy; and you of the Athenian Demus, and of Demus the son of Pyrilampes. Now, I observe that you, with all your cleverness, do not venture to contradict your favourite in any word or opinion of his; but as he changes you change, backwards and forwards. When the Athenian Demus denies anything that you are saying in the assembly, you go over to his opinion; and you do the same with Demus, the fair young son of Pyrilampes. For you have not the power to resist the words and ideas of your loves; and if a person were to express surprise at the strangeness of what you say from time to time when under their influence, you would probably reply to him, if you were honest, that you cannot help saying what your loves say unless they are prevented; and that you can only be silent when they are. Now you must understand that my words are an echo too, and therefore you need not wonder at me; but if you want to silence me, silence philosophy, who is my love, for she is always telling me what I am now telling you, my friend; neither is she capricious like my other love, for the son of Cleinias says one thing to-day and another thing to-morrow, but philosophy is always true. She is the teacher at whose words you are now wondering, and you have heard her yourself. Her you must refute, and either show, as I was saying, that to do injustice and to escape punishment is not the worst of all evils; or, if you leave her word unrefuted, by the dog the god of Egypt, I declare, O Callicles, that Callicles will never be at one with himself, but that his whole life will be a discord. And yet, my friend, I would rather that my lyre should be inharmonious, and that there should be no music in the chorus which I provided; aye, or that the whole world should be at odds with me, and oppose me, rather than that I myself should be at odds with myself, and contradict myself.

CALLICLES: O Socrates, you are a regular declaimer, and seem to be running riot in the argument. And now you are declaiming in this way because Polus has fallen into the same error himself of which he accused Gorgias:–for he said that when Gorgias was asked by you, whether, if some one came to him who wanted to learn rhetoric, and did not know justice, he would teach him justice, Gorgias in his modesty replied that he would, because he thought that mankind in general would be displeased if he answered "No"; and then in consequence of this admission, Gorgias was compelled to contradict himself, that being just the sort of thing in which you delight. Whereupon Polus laughed at you deservedly, as I think; but now he has himself fallen into the same trap. I cannot say very much for his wit when he conceded to you that to do is more dishonourable than to suffer injustice, for this was the admission which led to his being entangled by you; and because he was too modest to say what he thought, he had his mouth stopped. For the truth is, Socrates, that you, who pretend to be engaged in the pursuit of truth, are appealing now to the popular and vulgar notions of right, which are not natural, but only conventional. Convention and nature are generally at variance with one another: and hence, if a person is too modest to say what he thinks, he is compelled to contradict himself; and you, in your ingenuity perceiving the advantage to be thereby gained, slyly ask of him who is arguing conventionally a question which is to be determined by the rule of nature; and if he is talking of the rule of nature, you slip away to custom: as, for instance, you did in this very discussion about doing and suffering injustice. When Polus was speaking of the conventionally dishonourable, you assailed him from the point of view of nature; for by the rule of nature, to suffer injustice is the greater disgrace because the greater evil; but conventionally, to do evil is the more disgraceful. For the suffering of injustice is not the part of a man, but of a slave, who indeed had better die than live; since when he is wronged and trampled upon, he is unable to help himself, or any other about whom he cares. The reason, as I conceive, is that the makers of laws are the majority who are weak; and they make laws and distribute praises and censures with a view to themselves and to their own interests; and they terrify the stronger sort of men, and those who are able to get the better of them, in order that they may not get the better of them; and they say, that dishonesty is shameful and unjust; meaning, by the word injustice, the desire of a man to have more than his neighbours; for knowing their own inferiority, I suspect that they are too glad of equality. And therefore the endeavour to have more than the many, is conventionally said to be shameful and unjust, and is called injustice (compare Republic), whereas nature herself intimates that it is just for the better to have more than the worse, the more powerful than the weaker; and in many ways she shows, among men as well as among animals, and indeed among whole cities and races, that justice consists in the superior ruling over and having more than the inferior. For on what principle of justice did Xerxes invade Hellas, or his father the Scythians? (not to speak of numberless other examples). Nay, but these are the men who act according to nature; yes, by Heaven, and according to the law of nature: not, perhaps, according to that artificial law, which we invent and impose upon our fellows, of whom we take the best and strongest from their youth upwards, and tame them like young lions,–charming them with the sound of the voice, and saying to them, that with equality they must be content, and that the equal is the honourable and the just. But if there were a man who had sufficient force, he would shake off and break through, and escape from all this; he would trample under foot all our formulas and spells and charms, and all our laws which are against nature: the slave would rise in rebellion and be lord over us, and the light of natural justice would shine forth. And this I take to be the sentiment of Pindar, when he says in his poem, that

"Law is the king of all, of mortals as well as of immortals;" this, as he says,

"Makes might to be right, doing violence with highest hand; as I infer from the deeds of Heracles, for without buying them–" (Fragm. Incert. 151 (Bockh).) –I do not remember the exact words, but the meaning is, that without buying them, and without their being given to him, he carried off the oxen of Geryon, according to the law of natural right, and that the oxen and other possessions of the weaker and inferior properly belong to the stronger and superior. And this is true, as you may ascertain, if you will leave philosophy and go on to higher things: for philosophy, Socrates, if pursued in moderation and at the proper age, is an elegant accomplishment, but too much philosophy is the ruin of human life. Even if a man has good parts, still, if he carries philosophy into later life, he is necessarily ignorant of all those things which a gentleman and a person of honour ought to know; he is inexperienced in the laws of the State, and in the language which ought to be used in the dealings of man with man, whether private or public, and utterly ignorant of the pleasures and desires of mankind and of human character in general. And people of this sort, when they betake themselves to politics or business, are as ridiculous as I imagine the politicians to be, when they make their appearance in the arena of philosophy. For, as Euripides says,

"Every man shines in that and pursues that, and devotes the greatest portion of the day to that in which he most excels," (Antiope, fragm. 20 (Dindorf).)

but anything in which he is inferior, he avoids and depreciates, and praises the opposite from partiality to himself, and because he thinks that he will thus praise himself. The true principle is to unite them. Philosophy, as a part of education, is an excellent thing, and there is no disgrace to a man while he is young in pursuing such a study; but when he is more advanced in years, the thing becomes ridiculous, and I feel towards philosophers as I do towards those who lisp and imitate children. For I love to see a little child, who is not of an age to speak plainly, lisping at his play; there is an appearance of grace and freedom in his utterance, which is natural to his childish years. But when I hear some small creature carefully articulating its words, I am offended; the sound is disagreeable, and has to my ears the twang of slavery. So when I hear a man lisping, or see him playing like a child, his behaviour appears to me ridiculous and unmanly and worthy of stripes. And I have the same feeling about students of philosophy; when I see a youth thus engaged,–the study appears to me to be in character, and becoming a man of liberal education, and him who neglects philosophy I regard as an inferior man, who will never aspire to anything great or noble. But if I see him continuing the study in later life, and not leaving off, I should like to beat him, Socrates; for, as I was saying, such a one, even though he have good natural parts, becomes effeminate. He flies from the busy centre and the market-place, in which, as the poet says, men become distinguished; he creeps into a corner for the rest of his life, and talks in a whisper with three or four admiring youths, but never speaks out like a freeman in a satisfactory manner. Now I, Socrates, am very well inclined towards you, and my feeling may be compared with that of Zethus towards Amphion, in the play of Euripides, whom I was mentioning just now: for I am disposed to say to you much what Zethus said to his brother, that you, Socrates, are careless about the things of which you ought to be careful; and that you

"Who have a soul so noble, are remarkable for a puerile exterior; Neither in a court of justice could you state a case, or give any reason or proof, Or offer valiant counsel on another's behalf."

And you must not be offended, my dear Socrates, for I am speaking out of good-will towards you, if I ask whether you are not ashamed of being thus defenceless; which I affirm to be the condition not of you only but of all those who will carry the study of philosophy too far. For suppose that some one were to take you, or any one of your sort, off to prison, declaring that you had done wrong when you had done no wrong, you must allow that you would not know what to do:–there you would stand giddy and gaping, and not having a word to say; and when you went up before the Court, even if the accuser were a poor creature and not good for much, you would die if he were disposed to claim the penalty of death. And yet, Socrates, what is the value of

"An art which converts a man of sense into a fool,"

who is helpless, and has no power to save either himself or others, when he is in the greatest danger and is going to be despoiled by his enemies of all his goods, and has to live, simply deprived of his rights of citizenship?–he being a man who, if I may use the expression, may be boxed on the ears with impunity. Then, my good friend, take my advice, and refute no more:

"Learn the philosophy of business, and acquire the reputation of wisdom. But leave to others these niceties,"

whether they are to be described as follies or absurdities:

"For they will only Give you poverty for the inmate of your dwelling."

Cease, then, emulating these paltry splitters of words, and emulate only the man of substance and honour, who is well to do.

SOCRATES: If my soul, Callicles, were made of gold, should I not rejoice to discover one of those stones with which they test gold, and the very best possible one to which I might bring my soul; and if the stone and I agreed in approving of her training, then I should know that I was in a satisfactory state, and that no other test was needed by me.

CALLICLES: What is your meaning, Socrates?

SOCRATES: I will tell you; I think that I have found in you the desired touchstone.

CALLICLES: Why?

SOCRATES: Because I am sure that if you agree with me in any of the opinions which my soul forms, I have at last found the truth indeed. For I consider that if a man is to make a complete trial of the good or evil of the soul, he ought to have three qualities–knowledge, good-will, outspokenness, which are all possessed by you. Many whom I meet are unable to make trial of me, because they are not wise as you are; others are wise, but they will not tell me the truth, because they have not the same interest in me which you have; and these two strangers, Gorgias and Polus, are undoubtedly wise men and my very good friends, but they are not outspoken enough, and they are too modest. Why, their modesty is so great that they are driven to contradict themselves, first one and then the other of them, in the face of a large company, on matters of the highest moment. But you have all the qualities in which these others are deficient, having received an excellent education; to this many Athenians can testify. And you are my friend. Shall I tell you why I think so? I know that you, Callicles, and Tisander of Aphidnae, and Andron the son of Androtion, and Nausicydes of the deme of Cholarges, studied together: there were four of you, and I once heard you advising with one another as to the extent to which the pursuit of philosophy should be carried, and, as I know, you came to the conclusion that the study should not be pushed too much into detail. You were cautioning one another not to be overwise; you were afraid that too much wisdom might unconsciously to yourselves be the ruin of you. And now when I hear you giving the same advice to me which you then gave to your most intimate friends, I have a sufficient evidence of your real good-will to me. And of the frankness of your nature and freedom from modesty I am assured by yourself, and the assurance is confirmed by your last speech. Well then, the inference in the present case clearly is, that if you agree with me in an argument about any point, that point will have been sufficiently tested by us, and will not require to be submitted to any further test. For you could not have agreed with me, either from lack of knowledge or from superfluity of modesty, nor yet from a desire to deceive me, for you are my friend, as you tell me yourself. And therefore when you and I are agreed, the result will be the attainment of perfect truth. Now there is no nobler enquiry, Callicles, than that which you censure me for making,–What ought the character of a man to be, and what his pursuits, and how far is he to go, both in maturer years and in youth? For be assured that if I err in my own conduct I do not err intentionally, but from ignorance. Do not then desist from advising me, now that you have begun, until I have learned clearly what this is which I am to practise, and how I may acquire it. And if you find me assenting to your words, and hereafter not doing that to which I assented, call me "dolt," and deem me unworthy of receiving further instruction. Once more, then, tell me what you and Pindar mean by natural justice: Do you not mean that the superior should take the property of the inferior by force; that the better should rule the worse, the noble have more than the mean? Am I not right in my recollection?

CALLICLES: Yes; that is what I was saying, and so I still aver.

SOCRATES: And do you mean by the better the same as the superior? for I could not make out what you were saying at the time–whether you meant by the superior the stronger, and that the weaker must obey the stronger, as you seemed to imply when you said that great cities attack small ones in accordance with natural right, because they are superior and stronger, as though the superior and stronger and better were the same; or whether the better may be also the inferior and weaker, and the superior the worse, or whether better is to be defined in the same way as superior:– this is the point which I want to have cleared up. Are the superior and better and stronger the same or different?

CALLICLES: I say unequivocally that they are the same.

SOCRATES: Then the many are by nature superior to the one, against whom, as you were saying, they make the laws?

CALLICLES: Certainly.

SOCRATES: Then the laws of the many are the laws of the superior?

CALLICLES: Very true.

SOCRATES: Then they are the laws of the better; for the superior class are far better, as you were saying?

CALLICLES: Yes.

SOCRATES: And since they are superior, the laws which are made by them are by nature good?

CALLICLES: Yes.

SOCRATES: And are not the many of opinion, as you were lately saying, that justice is equality, and that to do is more disgraceful than to suffer injustice?–is that so or not? Answer, Callicles, and let no modesty be found to come in the way; do the many think, or do they not think thus?–I must beg of you to answer, in order that if you agree with me I may fortify myself by the assent of so competent an authority.

CALLICLES: Yes; the opinion of the many is what you say.

SOCRATES: Then not only custom but nature also affirms that to do is more disgraceful than to suffer injustice, and that justice is equality; so that you seem to have been wrong in your former assertion, when accusing me you said that nature and custom are opposed, and that I, knowing this, was dishonestly playing between them, appealing to custom when the argument is about nature, and to nature when the argument is about custom?

CALLICLES: This man will never cease talking nonsense. At your age, Socrates, are you not ashamed to be catching at words and chuckling over some verbal slip? do you not see–have I not told you already, that by superior I mean better: do you imagine me to say, that if a rabble of slaves and nondescripts, who are of no use except perhaps for their physical strength, get together, their ipsissima verba are laws?

SOCRATES: Ho! my philosopher, is that your line?

CALLICLES: Certainly.

SOCRATES: I was thinking, Callicles, that something of the kind must have been in your mind, and that is why I repeated the question,–What is the superior? I wanted to know clearly what you meant; for you surely do not think that two men are better than one, or that your slaves are better than you because they are stronger? Then please to begin again, and tell me who the better are, if they are not the stronger; and I will ask you, great Sir, to be a little milder in your instructions, or I shall have to run away from you.

CALLICLES: You are ironical.

SOCRATES: No, by the hero Zethus, Callicles, by whose aid you were just now saying many ironical things against me, I am not:–tell me, then, whom you mean, by the better?

CALLICLES: I mean the more excellent.

SOCRATES: Do you not see that you are yourself using words which have no meaning and that you are explaining nothing?–will you tell me whether you mean by the better and superior the wiser, or if not, whom?

CALLICLES: Most assuredly, I do mean the wiser.

SOCRATES: Then according to you, one wise man may often be superior to ten thousand fools, and he ought to rule them, and they ought to be his subjects, and he ought to have more than they should. This is what I believe that you mean (and you must not suppose that I am word-catching), if you allow that the one is superior to the ten thousand?

CALLICLES: Yes; that is what I mean, and that is what I conceive to be natural justice–that the better and wiser should rule and have more than the inferior.

SOCRATES: Stop there, and let me ask you what you would say in this case: Let us suppose that we are all together as we are now; there are several of us, and we have a large common store of meats and drinks, and there are all sorts of persons in our company having various degrees of strength and weakness, and one of us, being a physician, is wiser in the matter of food than all the rest, and he is probably stronger than some and not so strong as others of us–will he not, being wiser, be also better than we are, and our superior in this matter of food?

CALLICLES: Certainly.

SOCRATES: Either, then, he will have a larger share of the meats and drinks, because he is better, or he will have the distribution of all of them by reason of his authority, but he will not expend or make use of a larger share of them on his own person, or if he does, he will be punished;–his share will exceed that of some, and be less than that of others, and if he be the weakest of all, he being the best of all will have the smallest share of all, Callicles:–am I not right, my friend?

CALLICLES: You talk about meats and drinks and physicians and other nonsense; I am not speaking of them.

SOCRATES: Well, but do you admit that the wiser is the better? Answer "Yes" or "No."

CALLICLES: Yes.

SOCRATES: And ought not the better to have a larger share?

CALLICLES: Not of meats and drinks.

SOCRATES: I understand: then, perhaps, of coats–the skilfullest weaver ought to have the largest coat, and the greatest number of them, and go about clothed in the best and finest of them?

CALLICLES: Fudge about coats!

SOCRATES: Then the skilfullest and best in making shoes ought to have the advantage in shoes; the shoemaker, clearly, should walk about in the largest shoes, and have the greatest number of them?

CALLICLES: Fudge about shoes! What nonsense are you talking?

SOCRATES: Or, if this is not your meaning, perhaps you would say that the wise and good and true husbandman should actually have a larger share of seeds, and have as much seed as possible for his own land?

CALLICLES: How you go on, always talking in the same way, Socrates!

SOCRATES: Yes, Callicles, and also about the same things.

CALLICLES: Yes, by the Gods, you are literally always talking of cobblers and fullers and cooks and doctors, as if this had to do with our argument.

SOCRATES: But why will you not tell me in what a man must be superior and wiser in order to claim a larger share; will you neither accept a suggestion, nor offer one?

CALLICLES: I have already told you. In the first place, I mean by superiors not cobblers or cooks, but wise politicians who understand the administration of a state, and who are not only wise, but also valiant and able to carry out their designs, and not the men to faint from want of soul.

SOCRATES: See now, most excellent Callicles, how different my charge against you is from that which you bring against me, for you reproach me with always saying the same; but I reproach you with never saying the same about the same things, for at one time you were defining the better and the superior to be the stronger, then again as the wiser, and now you bring forward a new notion; the superior and the better are now declared by you to be the more courageous: I wish, my good friend, that you would tell me, once for all, whom you affirm to be the better and superior, and in what they are better?

CALLICLES: I have already told you that I mean those who are wise and courageous in the administration of a state–they ought to be the rulers of their states, and justice consists in their having more than their subjects.

SOCRATES: But whether rulers or subjects will they or will they not have more than themselves, my friend?

CALLICLES: What do you mean?

SOCRATES: I mean that every man is his own ruler; but perhaps you think that there is no necessity for him to rule himself; he is only required to rule others?

CALLICLES: What do you mean by his "ruling over himself"?

SOCRATES: A simple thing enough; just what is commonly said, that a man should be temperate and master of himself, and ruler of his own pleasures and passions.

CALLICLES: What innocence! you mean those fools,–the temperate?

SOCRATES: Certainly:–any one may know that to be my meaning.

CALLICLES: Quite so, Socrates; and they are really fools, for how can a man be happy who is the servant of anything? On the contrary, I plainly assert, that he who would truly live ought to allow his desires to wax to the uttermost, and not to chastise them; but when they have grown to their greatest he should have courage and intelligence to minister to them and to satisfy all his longings. And this I affirm to be natural justice and nobility. To this however the many cannot attain; and they blame the strong man because they are ashamed of their own weakness, which they desire to conceal, and hence they say that intemperance is base. As I have remarked already, they enslave the nobler natures, and being unable to satisfy their pleasures, they praise temperance and justice out of their own cowardice. For if a man had been originally the son of a king, or had a nature capable of acquiring an empire or a tyranny or sovereignty, what could be more truly base or evil than temperance–to a man like him, I say, who might freely be enjoying every good, and has no one to stand in his way, and yet has admitted custom and reason and the opinion of other men to be lords over him?–must not he be in a miserable plight whom the reputation of justice and temperance hinders from giving more to his friends than to his enemies, even though he be a ruler in his city? Nay, Socrates, for you profess to be a votary of the truth, and the truth is this:–that luxury and intemperance and licence, if they be provided with means, are virtue and happiness–all the rest is a mere bauble, agreements contrary to nature, foolish talk of men, nothing worth. (Compare Republic.)

SOCRATES: There is a noble freedom, Callicles, in your way of approaching the argument; for what you say is what the rest of the world think, but do not like to say. And I must beg of you to persevere, that the true rule of human life may become manifest. Tell me, then:–you say, do you not, that in the rightly-developed man the passions ought not to be controlled, but that we should let them grow to the utmost and somehow or other satisfy them, and that this is virtue?

CALLICLES: Yes; I do.

SOCRATES: Then those who want nothing are not truly said to be happy?

CALLICLES: No indeed, for then stones and dead men would be the happiest of all.

SOCRATES: But surely life according to your view is an awful thing; and indeed I think that Euripides may have been right in saying,

"Who knows if life be not death and death life;"

and that we are very likely dead; I have heard a philosopher say that at this moment we are actually dead, and that the body (soma) is our tomb (sema (compare Phaedr.)), and that the part of the soul which is the seat of the desires is liable to be tossed about by words and blown up and down; and some ingenious person, probably a Sicilian or an Italian, playing with the word, invented a tale in which he called the soul–because of its believing and make-believe nature–a vessel (An untranslatable pun,–dia to pithanon te kai pistikon onomase pithon.), and the ignorant he called the uninitiated or leaky, and the place in the souls of the uninitiated in which the desires are seated, being the intemperate and incontinent part, he compared to a vessel full of holes, because it can never be satisfied. He is not of your way of thinking, Callicles, for he declares, that of all the souls in Hades, meaning the invisible world (aeides), these uninitiated or leaky persons are the most miserable, and that they pour water into a vessel which is full of holes out of a colander which is similarly perforated. The colander, as my informer assures me, is the soul, and the soul which he compares to a colander is the soul of the ignorant, which is likewise full of holes, and therefore incontinent, owing to a bad memory and want of faith. These notions are strange enough, but they show the principle which, if I can, I would fain prove to you; that you should change your mind, and, instead of the intemperate and insatiate life, choose that which is orderly and sufficient and has a due provision for daily needs. Do I make any impression on you, and are you coming over to the opinion that the orderly are happier than the intemperate? Or do I fail to persuade you, and, however many tales I rehearse to you, do you continue of the same opinion still?

CALLICLES: The latter, Socrates, is more like the truth.

SOCRATES: Well, I will tell you another image, which comes out of the same school:–Let me request you to consider how far you would accept this as an account of the two lives of the temperate and intemperate in a figure:–There are two men, both of whom have a number of casks; the one man has his casks sound and full, one of wine, another of honey, and a third of milk, besides others filled with other liquids, and the streams which fill them are few and scanty, and he can only obtain them with a great deal of toil and difficulty; but when his casks are once filled he has no need to feed them any more, and has no further trouble with them or care about them. The other, in like manner, can procure streams, though not without difficulty; but his vessels are leaky and unsound, and night and day he is compelled to be filling them, and if he pauses for a moment, he is in an agony of pain. Such are their respective lives:–And now would you say that the life of the intemperate is happier than that of the temperate? Do I not convince you that the opposite is the truth?

CALLICLES: You do not convince me, Socrates, for the one who has filled himself has no longer any pleasure left; and this, as I was just now saying, is the life of a stone: he has neither joy nor sorrow after he is once filled; but the pleasure depends on the superabundance of the influx.

SOCRATES: But the more you pour in, the greater the waste; and the holes must be large for the liquid to escape.

CALLICLES: Certainly.

SOCRATES: The life which you are now depicting is not that of a dead man, or of a stone, but of a cormorant; you mean that he is to be hungering and eating?

CALLICLES: Yes.

SOCRATES: And he is to be thirsting and drinking?

CALLICLES: Yes, that is what I mean; he is to have all his desires about him, and to be able to live happily in the gratification of them.

SOCRATES: Capital, excellent; go on as you have begun, and have no shame; I, too, must disencumber myself of shame: and first, will you tell me whether you include itching and scratching, provided you have enough of them and pass your life in scratching, in your notion of happiness?

CALLICLES: What a strange being you are, Socrates! a regular mob-orator.

SOCRATES: That was the reason, Callicles, why I scared Polus and Gorgias, until they were too modest to say what they thought; but you will not be too modest and will not be scared, for you are a brave man. And now, answer my question.

CALLICLES: I answer, that even the scratcher would live pleasantly.

SOCRATES: And if pleasantly, then also happily?

CALLICLES: To be sure.

SOCRATES: But what if the itching is not confined to the head? Shall I pursue the question? And here, Callicles, I would have you consider how you would reply if consequences are pressed upon you, especially if in the last resort you are asked, whether the life of a catamite is not terrible, foul, miserable? Or would you venture to say, that they too are happy, if they only get enough of what they want?

CALLICLES: Are you not ashamed, Socrates, of introducing such topics into the argument?

SOCRATES: Well, my fine friend, but am I the introducer of these topics, or he who says without any qualification that all who feel pleasure in whatever manner are happy, and who admits of no distinction between good and bad pleasures? And I would still ask, whether you say that pleasure and good are the same, or whether there is some pleasure which is not a good?

CALLICLES: Well, then, for the sake of consistency, I will say that they are the same.

SOCRATES: You are breaking the original agreement, Callicles, and will no longer be a satisfactory companion in the search after truth, if you say what is contrary to your real opinion.

CALLICLES: Why, that is what you are doing too, Socrates.

SOCRATES: Then we are both doing wrong. Still, my dear friend, I would ask you to consider whether pleasure, from whatever source derived, is the good; for, if this be true, then the disagreeable consequences which have been darkly intimated must follow, and many others.

CALLICLES: That, Socrates, is only your opinion.

SOCRATES: And do you, Callicles, seriously maintain what you are saying?

CALLICLES: Indeed I do.

SOCRATES: Then, as you are in earnest, shall we proceed with the argument?

CALLICLES: By all means. (Or, "I am in profound earnest.")

SOCRATES: Well, if you are willing to proceed, determine this question for me:–There is something, I presume, which you would call knowledge?

CALLICLES: There is.

SOCRATES: And were you not saying just now, that some courage implied knowledge?

CALLICLES: I was.

SOCRATES: And you were speaking of courage and knowledge as two things different from one another?

CALLICLES: Certainly I was.

SOCRATES: And would you say that pleasure and knowledge are the same, or not the same?

CALLICLES: Not the same, O man of wisdom.

SOCRATES: And would you say that courage differed from pleasure?

CALLICLES: Certainly.

SOCRATES: Well, then, let us remember that Callicles, the Acharnian, says that pleasure and good are the same; but that knowledge and courage are not the same, either with one another, or with the good.

CALLICLES: And what does our friend Socrates, of Foxton, say–does he assent to this, or not?

SOCRATES: He does not assent; neither will Callicles, when he sees himself truly. You will admit, I suppose, that good and evil fortune are opposed to each other?

CALLICLES: Yes.

SOCRATES: And if they are opposed to each other, then, like health and disease, they exclude one another; a man cannot have them both, or be without them both, at the same time?

CALLICLES: What do you mean?

SOCRATES: Take the case of any bodily affection:–a man may have the complaint in his eyes which is called ophthalmia?

CALLICLES: To be sure.

SOCRATES: But he surely cannot have the same eyes well and sound at the same time?

CALLICLES: Certainly not.

SOCRATES: And when he has got rid of his ophthalmia, has he got rid of the health of his eyes too? Is the final result, that he gets rid of them both together?

CALLICLES: Certainly not.

SOCRATES: That would surely be marvellous and absurd?

CALLICLES: Very.

SOCRATES: I suppose that he is affected by them, and gets rid of them in turns?

CALLICLES: Yes.

SOCRATES: And he may have strength and weakness in the same way, by fits?

CALLICLES: Yes.

SOCRATES: Or swiftness and slowness?

CALLICLES: Certainly.

SOCRATES: And does he have and not have good and happiness, and their opposites, evil and misery, in a similar alternation? (Compare Republic.)

CALLICLES: Certainly he has.

SOCRATES: If then there be anything which a man has and has not at the same time, clearly that cannot be good and evil–do we agree? Please not to answer without consideration.

CALLICLES: I entirely agree.

SOCRATES: Go back now to our former admissions.–Did you say that to hunger, I mean the mere state of hunger, was pleasant or painful?

CALLICLES: I said painful, but that to eat when you are hungry is pleasant.

SOCRATES: I know; but still the actual hunger is painful: am I not right?

CALLICLES: Yes.

SOCRATES: And thirst, too, is painful?

CALLICLES: Yes, very.

SOCRATES: Need I adduce any more instances, or would you agree that all wants or desires are painful?

CALLICLES: I agree, and therefore you need not adduce any more instances.

SOCRATES: Very good. And you would admit that to drink, when you are thirsty, is pleasant?

CALLICLES: Yes.

SOCRATES: And in the sentence which you have just uttered, the word "thirsty" implies pain?

CALLICLES: Yes.

SOCRATES: And the word "drinking" is expressive of pleasure, and of the satisfaction of the want?

CALLICLES: Yes.

SOCRATES: There is pleasure in drinking?

CALLICLES: Certainly.

SOCRATES: When you are thirsty?

SOCRATES: And in pain?

CALLICLES: Yes.

SOCRATES: Do you see the inference:–that pleasure and pain are simultaneous, when you say that being thirsty, you drink? For are they not simultaneous, and do they not affect at the same time the same part, whether of the soul or the body?–which of them is affected cannot be supposed to be of any consequence: Is not this true?

CALLICLES: It is.

SOCRATES: You said also, that no man could have good and evil fortune at the same time?

CALLICLES: Yes, I did.

SOCRATES: But you admitted, that when in pain a man might also have pleasure?

CALLICLES: Clearly.

SOCRATES: Then pleasure is not the same as good fortune, or pain the same as evil fortune, and therefore the good is not the same as the pleasant?

CALLICLES: I wish I knew, Socrates, what your quibbling means.

SOCRATES: You know, Callicles, but you affect not to know.

CALLICLES: Well, get on, and don't keep fooling: then you will know what a wiseacre you are in your admonition of me.

SOCRATES: Does not a man cease from his thirst and from his pleasure in drinking at the same time?

CALLICLES: I do not understand what you are saying.

GORGIAS: Nay, Callicles, answer, if only for our sakes;–we should like to hear the argument out.

CALLICLES: Yes, Gorgias, but I must complain of the habitual trifling of Socrates; he is always arguing about little and unworthy questions.

GORGIAS: What matter? Your reputation, Callicles, is not at stake. Let Socrates argue in his own fashion.

CALLICLES: Well, then, Socrates, you shall ask these little peddling questions, since Gorgias wishes to have them.

SOCRATES: I envy you, Callicles, for having been initiated into the great mysteries before you were initiated into the lesser. I thought that this was not allowable. But to return to our argument:–Does not a man cease from thirsting and from the pleasure of drinking at the same moment?

CALLICLES: True.

SOCRATES: And if he is hungry, or has any other desire, does he not cease from the desire and the pleasure at the same moment?

CALLICLES: Very true.

SOCRATES: Then he ceases from pain and pleasure at the same moment?

CALLICLES: Yes.

SOCRATES: But he does not cease from good and evil at the same moment, as you have admitted: do you still adhere to what you said?

CALLICLES: Yes, I do; but what is the inference?

SOCRATES: Why, my friend, the inference is that the good is not the same as the pleasant, or the evil the same as the painful; there is a cessation of pleasure and pain at the same moment; but not of good and evil, for they are different. How then can pleasure be the same as good, or pain as evil? And I would have you look at the matter in another light, which could hardly, I think, have been considered by you when you identified them: Are not the good good because they have good present with them, as the beautiful are those who have beauty present with them?

CALLICLES: Yes.

SOCRATES: And do you call the fools and cowards good men? For you were saying just now that the courageous and the wise are the good–would you not say so?

CALLICLES: Certainly.

SOCRATES: And did you never see a foolish child rejoicing?

CALLICLES: Yes, I have.

SOCRATES: And a foolish man too?

CALLICLES: Yes, certainly; but what is your drift?

SOCRATES: Nothing particular, if you will only answer.

CALLICLES: Yes, I have.

SOCRATES: And did you ever see a sensible man rejoicing or sorrowing?

CALLICLES: Yes.

SOCRATES: Which rejoice and sorrow most–the wise or the foolish?

CALLICLES: They are much upon a par, I think, in that respect.

SOCRATES: Enough: And did you ever see a coward in battle?

CALLICLES: To be sure.

SOCRATES: And which rejoiced most at the departure of the enemy, the coward or the brave?

CALLICLES: I should say "most" of both; or at any rate, they rejoiced about equally.

SOCRATES: No matter; then the cowards, and not only the brave, rejoice?

CALLICLES: Greatly.

SOCRATES: And the foolish; so it would seem?

CALLICLES: Yes.

SOCRATES: And are only the cowards pained at the approach of their enemies, or are the brave also pained?

CALLICLES: Both are pained.

SOCRATES: And are they equally pained?

CALLICLES: I should imagine that the cowards are more pained.

SOCRATES: And are they not better pleased at the enemy's departure?

CALLICLES: I dare say.

SOCRATES: Then are the foolish and the wise and the cowards and the brave all pleased and pained, as you were saying, in nearly equal degree; but are the cowards more pleased and pained than the brave?

CALLICLES: Yes.

SOCRATES: But surely the wise and brave are the good, and the foolish and the cowardly are the bad?

CALLICLES: Yes.

SOCRATES: Then the good and the bad are pleased and pained in a nearly equal degree?

CALLICLES: Yes.

SOCRATES: Then are the good and bad good and bad in a nearly equal degree, or have the bad the advantage both in good and evil? (i.e. in having more pleasure and more pain.)

CALLICLES: I really do not know what you mean.

SOCRATES: Why, do you not remember saying that the good were good because good was present with them, and the evil because evil; and that pleasures were goods and pains evils?

CALLICLES: Yes, I remember.

SOCRATES: And are not these pleasures or goods present to those who rejoice–if they do rejoice?

CALLICLES: Certainly.

SOCRATES: Then those who rejoice are good when goods are present with them?

CALLICLES: Yes.

SOCRATES: And those who are in pain have evil or sorrow present with them?

CALLICLES: Yes.

SOCRATES: And would you still say that the evil are evil by reason of the presence of evil?

CALLICLES: I should.

SOCRATES: Then those who rejoice are good, and those who are in pain evil?

CALLICLES: Yes.

SOCRATES: The degrees of good and evil vary with the degrees of pleasure and of pain?

CALLICLES: Yes.

SOCRATES: Have the wise man and the fool, the brave and the coward, joy and pain in nearly equal degrees? or would you say that the coward has more?

CALLICLES: I should say that he has.

SOCRATES: Help me then to draw out the conclusion which follows from our admissions; for it is good to repeat and review what is good twice and thrice over, as they say. Both the wise man and the brave man we allow to be good?

CALLICLES: Yes.

SOCRATES: And the foolish man and the coward to be evil?

CALLICLES: Certainly.

SOCRATES: And he who has joy is good?

CALLICLES: Yes.

SOCRATES: And he who is in pain is evil?

CALLICLES: Certainly.

SOCRATES: The good and evil both have joy and pain, but, perhaps, the evil has more of them?

CALLICLES: Yes.

SOCRATES: Then must we not infer, that the bad man is as good and bad as the good, or, perhaps, even better?–is not this a further inference which follows equally with the preceding from the assertion that the good and the pleasant are the same:–can this be denied, Callicles?

CALLICLES: I have been listening and making admissions to you, Socrates; and I remark that if a person grants you anything in play, you, like a child, want to keep hold and will not give it back. But do you really suppose that I or any other human being denies that some pleasures are good and others bad?

SOCRATES: Alas, Callicles, how unfair you are! you certainly treat me as if I were a child, sometimes saying one thing, and then another, as if you were meaning to deceive me. And yet I thought at first that you were my friend, and would not have deceived me if you could have helped. But I see that I was mistaken; and now I suppose that I must make the best of a bad business, as they said of old, and take what I can get out of you.–Well, then, as I understand you to say, I may assume that some pleasures are good and others evil?

CALLICLES: Yes.

SOCRATES: The beneficial are good, and the hurtful are evil?

CALLICLES: To be sure.

SOCRATES: And the beneficial are those which do some good, and the hurtful are those which do some evil?

CALLICLES: Yes.

SOCRATES: Take, for example, the bodily pleasures of eating and drinking, which we were just now mentioning–you mean to say that those which promote health, or any other bodily excellence, are good, and their opposites evil?

CALLICLES: Certainly.

SOCRATES: And in the same way there are good pains and there are evil pains?

CALLICLES: To be sure.

SOCRATES: And ought we not to choose and use the good pleasures and pains?

CALLICLES: Certainly.

SOCRATES: But not the evil?

CALLICLES: Clearly.

SOCRATES: Because, if you remember, Polus and I have agreed that all our actions are to be done for the sake of the good;–and will you agree with us in saying, that the good is the end of all our actions, and that all our actions are to be done for the sake of the good, and not the good for the sake of them?–will you add a third vote to our two?

CALLICLES: I will.

SOCRATES: Then pleasure, like everything else, is to be sought for the sake of that which is good, and not that which is good for the sake of pleasure?

CALLICLES: To be sure.

SOCRATES: But can every man choose what pleasures are good and what are evil, or must he have art or knowledge of them in detail?

CALLICLES: He must have art.

SOCRATES: Let me now remind you of what I was saying to Gorgias and Polus; I was saying, as you will not have forgotten, that there were some processes which aim only at pleasure, and know nothing of a better and worse, and there are other processes which know good and evil. And I considered that cookery, which I do not call an art, but only an experience, was of the former class, which is concerned with pleasure, and that the art of medicine was of the class which is concerned with the good. And now, by the god of friendship, I must beg you, Callicles, not to jest, or to imagine that I am jesting with you; do not answer at random and contrary to your real opinion–for you will observe that we are arguing about the way of human life; and to a man who has any sense at all, what question can be more serious than this?–whether he should follow after that way of life to which you exhort me, and act what you call the manly part of speaking in the assembly, and cultivating rhetoric, and engaging in public affairs, according to the principles now in vogue; or whether he should pursue the life of philosophy;– and in what the latter way differs from the former. But perhaps we had better first try to distinguish them, as I did before, and when we have come to an agreement that they are distinct, we may proceed to consider in what they differ from one another, and which of them we should choose. Perhaps, however, you do not even now understand what I mean?

CALLICLES: No, I do not.

SOCRATES: Then I will explain myself more clearly: seeing that you and I have agreed that there is such a thing as good, and that there is such a thing as pleasure, and that pleasure is not the same as good, and that the pursuit and process of acquisition of the one, that is pleasure, is different from the pursuit and process of acquisition of the other, which is good–I wish that you would tell me whether you agree with me thus far or not–do you agree?

CALLICLES: I do.

SOCRATES: Then I will proceed, and ask whether you also agree with me, and whether you think that I spoke the truth when I further said to Gorgias and Polus that cookery in my opinion is only an experience, and not an art at all; and that whereas medicine is an art, and attends to the nature and constitution of the patient, and has principles of action and reason in each case, cookery in attending upon pleasure never regards either the nature or reason of that pleasure to which she devotes herself, but goes straight to her end, nor ever considers or calculates anything, but works by experience and routine, and just preserves the recollection of what she has usually done when producing pleasure. And first, I would have you consider whether I have proved what I was saying, and then whether there are not other similar processes which have to do with the soul–some of them processes of art, making a provision for the soul's highest interest–others despising the interest, and, as in the previous case, considering only the pleasure of the soul, and how this may be acquired, but not considering what pleasures are good or bad, and having no other aim but to afford gratification, whether good or bad. In my opinion, Callicles, there are such processes, and this is the sort of thing which I term flattery, whether concerned with the body or the soul, or whenever employed with a view to pleasure and without any consideration of good and evil. And now I wish that you would tell me whether you agree with us in this notion, or whether you differ.

CALLICLES: I do not differ; on the contrary, I agree; for in that way I shall soonest bring the argument to an end, and shall oblige my friend Gorgias.

SOCRATES: And is this notion true of one soul, or of two or more?

CALLICLES: Equally true of two or more.

SOCRATES: Then a man may delight a whole assembly, and yet have no regard for their true interests?

CALLICLES: Yes.

SOCRATES: Can you tell me the pursuits which delight mankind–or rather, if you would prefer, let me ask, and do you answer, which of them belong to the pleasurable class, and which of them not? In the first place, what say you of flute-playing? Does not that appear to be an art which seeks only pleasure, Callicles, and thinks of nothing else?

CALLICLES: I assent.

SOCRATES: And is not the same true of all similar arts, as, for example, the art of playing the lyre at festivals?

CALLICLES: Yes.

SOCRATES: And what do you say of the choral art and of dithyrambic poetry?–are not they of the same nature? Do you imagine that Cinesias the son of Meles cares about what will tend to the moral improvement of his hearers, or about what will give pleasure to the multitude?

CALLICLES: There can be no mistake about Cinesias, Socrates.

SOCRATES: And what do you say of his father, Meles the harp-player? Did he perform with any view to the good of his hearers? Could he be said to regard even their pleasure? For his singing was an infliction to his audience. And of harp-playing and dithyrambic poetry in general, what would you say? Have they not been invented wholly for the sake of pleasure?

CALLICLES: That is my notion of them.

SOCRATES: And as for the Muse of Tragedy, that solemn and august personage–what are her aspirations? Is all her aim and desire only to give pleasure to the spectators, or does she fight against them and refuse to speak of their pleasant vices, and willingly proclaim in word and song truths welcome and unwelcome?–which in your judgment is her character?

CALLICLES: There can be no doubt, Socrates, that Tragedy has her face turned towards pleasure and the gratification of the audience.

SOCRATES: And is not that the sort of thing, Callicles, which we were just now describing as flattery?

CALLICLES: Quite true.

SOCRATES: Well now, suppose that we strip all poetry of song and rhythm and metre, there will remain speech? (Compare Republic.)

CALLICLES: To be sure.

SOCRATES: And this speech is addressed to a crowd of people?

CALLICLES: Yes.

SOCRATES: Then poetry is a sort of rhetoric?

CALLICLES: True.

SOCRATES: And do not the poets in the theatres seem to you to be rhetoricians?

CALLICLES: Yes.

SOCRATES: Then now we have discovered a sort of rhetoric which is addressed to a crowd of men, women, and children, freemen and slaves. And this is not much to our taste, for we have described it as having the nature of flattery.

CALLICLES: Quite true.

SOCRATES: Very good. And what do you say of that other rhetoric which addresses the Athenian assembly and the assemblies of freemen in other states? Do the rhetoricians appear to you always to aim at what is best, and do they seek to improve the citizens by their speeches, or are they too, like the rest of mankind, bent upon giving them pleasure, forgetting the public good in the thought of their own interest, playing with the people as with children, and trying to amuse them, but never considering whether they are better or worse for this?

CALLICLES: I must distinguish. There are some who have a real care of the public in what they say, while others are such as you describe.

SOCRATES: I am contented with the admission that rhetoric is of two sorts; one, which is mere flattery and disgraceful declamation; the other, which is noble and aims at the training and improvement of the souls of the citizens, and strives to say what is best, whether welcome or unwelcome, to the audience; but have you ever known such a rhetoric; or if you have, and can point out any rhetorician who is of this stamp, who is he?

CALLICLES: But, indeed, I am afraid that I cannot tell you of any such among the orators who are at present living.

SOCRATES: Well, then, can you mention any one of a former generation, who may be said to have improved the Athenians, who found them worse and made them better, from the day that he began to make speeches? for, indeed, I do not know of such a man.

CALLICLES: What! did you never hear that Themistocles was a good man, and Cimon and Miltiades and Pericles, who is just lately dead, and whom you heard yourself?

SOCRATES: Yes, Callicles, they were good men, if, as you said at first, true virtue consists only in the satisfaction of our own desires and those of others; but if not, and if, as we were afterwards compelled to acknowledge, the satisfaction of some desires makes us better, and of others, worse, and we ought to gratify the one and not the other, and there is an art in distinguishing them,–can you tell me of any of these statesmen who did distinguish them?

CALLICLES: No, indeed, I cannot.

SOCRATES: Yet, surely, Callicles, if you look you will find such a one. Suppose that we just calmly consider whether any of these was such as I have described. Will not the good man, who says whatever he says with a view to the best, speak with a reference to some standard and not at random; just as all other artists, whether the painter, the builder, the shipwright, or any other look all of them to their own work, and do not select and apply at random what they apply, but strive to give a definite form to it? The artist disposes all things in order, and compels the one part to harmonize and accord with the other part, until he has constructed a regular and systematic whole; and this is true of all artists, and in the same way the trainers and physicians, of whom we spoke before, give order and regularity to the body: do you deny this?

CALLICLES: No; I am ready to admit it.

SOCRATES: Then the house in which order and regularity prevail is good; that in which there is disorder, evil?

CALLICLES: Yes.

SOCRATES: And the same is true of a ship?

CALLICLES: Yes.

SOCRATES: And the same may be said of the human body?

CALLICLES: Yes.

SOCRATES: And what would you say of the soul? Will the good soul be that in which disorder is prevalent, or that in which there is harmony and order?

CALLICLES: The latter follows from our previous admissions.

SOCRATES: What is the name which is given to the effect of harmony and order in the body?

CALLICLES: I suppose that you mean health and strength?

SOCRATES: Yes, I do; and what is the name which you would give to the effect of harmony and order in the soul? Try and discover a name for this as well as for the other.

CALLICLES: Why not give the name yourself, Socrates?

SOCRATES: Well, if you had rather that I should, I will; and you shall say whether you agree with me, and if not, you shall refute and answer me. "Healthy," as I conceive, is the name which is given to the regular order of the body, whence comes health and every other bodily excellence: is that true or not?

CALLICLES: True.

SOCRATES: And "lawful" and "law" are the names which are given to the regular order and action of the soul, and these make men lawful and orderly:–and so we have temperance and justice: have we not?

CALLICLES: Granted.

SOCRATES: And will not the true rhetorician who is honest and understands his art have his eye fixed upon these, in all the words which he addresses to the souls of men, and in all his actions, both in what he gives and in what he takes away? Will not his aim be to implant justice in the souls of his citizens and take away injustice, to implant temperance and take away intemperance, to implant every virtue and take away every vice? Do you not agree?

CALLICLES: I agree.

SOCRATES: For what use is there, Callicles, in giving to the body of a sick man who is in a bad state of health a quantity of the most delightful food or drink or any other pleasant thing, which may be really as bad for him as if you gave him nothing, or even worse if rightly estimated. Is not that true?

CALLICLES: I will not say No to it.

SOCRATES: For in my opinion there is no profit in a man's life if his body is in an evil plight–in that case his life also is evil: am I not right?

CALLICLES: Yes.

SOCRATES: When a man is in health the physicians will generally allow him to eat when he is hungry and drink when he is thirsty, and to satisfy his desires as he likes, but when he is sick they hardly suffer him to satisfy his desires at all: even you will admit that?

CALLICLES: Yes.

SOCRATES: And does not the same argument hold of the soul, my good sir? While she is in a bad state and is senseless and intemperate and unjust and unholy, her desires ought to be controlled, and she ought to be prevented from doing anything which does not tend to her own improvement.

CALLICLES: Yes.

SOCRATES: Such treatment will be better for the soul herself?

CALLICLES: To be sure.

SOCRATES: And to restrain her from her appetites is to chastise her?

CALLICLES: Yes.

SOCRATES: Then restraint or chastisement is better for the soul than intemperance or the absence of control, which you were just now preferring?

CALLICLES: I do not understand you, Socrates, and I wish that you would ask some one who does.

SOCRATES: Here is a gentleman who cannot endure to be improved or to subject himself to that very chastisement of which the argument speaks!

CALLICLES: I do not heed a word of what you are saying, and have only answered hitherto out of civility to Gorgias.

SOCRATES: What are we to do, then? Shall we break off in the middle?

CALLICLES: You shall judge for yourself.

SOCRATES: Well, but people say that "a tale should have a head and not break off in the middle," and I should not like to have the argument going about without a head (compare Laws); please then to go on a little longer, and put the head on.

CALLICLES: How tyrannical you are, Socrates! I wish that you and your argument would rest, or that you would get some one else to argue with you.

SOCRATES: But who else is willing?–I want to finish the argument.

CALLICLES: Cannot you finish without my help, either talking straight on, or questioning and answering yourself?

SOCRATES: Must I then say with Epicharmus, "Two men spoke before, but now one shall be enough"? I suppose that there is absolutely no help. And if I am to carry on the enquiry by myself, I will first of all remark that not only I but all of us should have an ambition to know what is true and what is false in this matter, for the discovery of the truth is a common good. And now I will proceed to argue according to my own notion. But if any of you think that I arrive at conclusions which are untrue you must interpose and refute me, for I do not speak from any knowledge of what I am saying; I am an enquirer like yourselves, and therefore, if my opponent says anything which is of force, I shall be the first to agree with him. I am speaking on the supposition that the argument ought to be completed; but if you think otherwise let us leave off and go our ways.

GORGIAS: I think, Socrates, that we should not go our ways until you have completed the argument; and this appears to me to be the wish of the rest of the company; I myself should very much like to hear what more you have to say.

SOCRATES: I too, Gorgias, should have liked to continue the argument with Callicles, and then I might have given him an "Amphion" in return for his "Zethus"; but since you, Callicles, are unwilling to continue, I hope that you will listen, and interrupt me if I seem to you to be in error. And if you refute me, I shall not be angry with you as you are with me, but I shall inscribe you as the greatest of benefactors on the tablets of my soul.

CALLICLES: My good fellow, never mind me, but get on.

SOCRATES: Listen to me, then, while I recapitulate the argument:–Is the pleasant the same as the good? Not the same. Callicles and I are agreed about that. And is the pleasant to be pursued for the sake of the good? or the good for the sake of the pleasant? The pleasant is to be pursued for the sake of the good. And that is pleasant at the presence of which we are pleased, and that is good at the presence of which we are good? To be sure. And we are good, and all good things whatever are good when some virtue is present in us or them? That, Callicles, is my conviction. But the virtue of each thing, whether body or soul, instrument or creature, when given to them in the best way comes to them not by chance but as the result of the order and truth and art which are imparted to them: Am I not right? I maintain that I am. And is not the virtue of each thing dependent on order or arrangement? Yes, I say. And that which makes a thing good is the proper order inhering in each thing? Such is my view. And is not the soul which has an order of her own better than that which has no order? Certainly. And the soul which has order is orderly? Of course. And that which is orderly is temperate? Assuredly. And the temperate soul is good? No other answer can I give, Callicles dear; have you any?

CALLICLES: Go on, my good fellow.

SOCRATES: Then I shall proceed to add, that if the temperate soul is the good soul, the soul which is in the opposite condition, that is, the foolish and intemperate, is the bad soul. Very true.

And will not the temperate man do what is proper, both in relation to the gods and to men;–for he would not be temperate if he did not? Certainly he will do what is proper. In his relation to other men he will do what is just; and in his relation to the gods he will do what is holy; and he who does what is just and holy must be just and holy? Very true. And must he not be courageous? for the duty of a temperate man is not to follow or to avoid what he ought not, but what he ought, whether things or men or pleasures or pains, and patiently to endure when he ought; and therefore, Callicles, the temperate man, being, as we have described, also just and courageous and holy, cannot be other than a perfectly good man, nor can the good man do otherwise than well and perfectly whatever he does; and he who does well must of necessity be happy and blessed, and the evil man who does evil, miserable: now this latter is he whom you were applauding–the intemperate who is the opposite of the temperate. Such is my position, and these things I affirm to be true. And if they are true, then I further affirm that he who desires to be happy must pursue and practise temperance and run away from intemperance as fast as his legs will carry him: he had better order his life so as not to need punishment; but if either he or any of his friends, whether private individual or city, are in need of punishment, then justice must be done and he must suffer punishment, if he would be happy. This appears to me to be the aim which a man ought to have, and towards which he ought to direct all the energies both of himself and of the state, acting so that he may have temperance and justice present with him and be happy, not suffering his lusts to be unrestrained, and in the never-ending desire satisfy them leading a robber's life. Such a one is the friend neither of God nor man, for he is incapable of communion, and he who is incapable of communion is also incapable of friendship. And philosophers tell us, Callicles, that communion and friendship and orderliness and temperance and justice bind together heaven and earth and gods and men, and that this universe is therefore called Cosmos or order, not disorder or misrule, my friend. But although you are a philosopher you seem to me never to have observed that geometrical equality is mighty, both among gods and men; you think that you ought to cultivate inequality or excess, and do not care about geometry.–Well, then, either the principle that the happy are made happy by the possession of justice and temperance, and the miserable miserable by the possession of vice, must be refuted, or, if it is granted, what will be the consequences? All the consequences which I drew before, Callicles, and about which you asked me whether I was in earnest when I said that a man ought to accuse himself and his son and his friend if he did anything wrong, and that to this end he should use his rhetoric–all those consequences are true. And that which you thought that Polus was led to admit out of modesty is true, viz., that, to do injustice, if more disgraceful than to suffer, is in that degree worse; and the other position, which, according to Polus, Gorgias admitted out of modesty, that he who would truly be a rhetorician ought to be just and have a knowledge of justice, has also turned out to be true.

And now, these things being as we have said, let us proceed in the next place to consider whether you are right in throwing in my teeth that I am unable to help myself or any of my friends or kinsmen, or to save them in the extremity of danger, and that I am in the power of another like an outlaw to whom any one may do what he likes,–he may box my ears, which was a brave saying of yours; or take away my goods or banish me, or even do his worst and kill me; a condition which, as you say, is the height of disgrace. My answer to you is one which has been already often repeated, but may as well be repeated once more. I tell you, Callicles, that to be boxed on the ears wrongfully is not the worst evil which can befall a man, nor to have my purse or my body cut open, but that to smite and slay me and mine wrongfully is far more disgraceful and more evil; aye, and to despoil and enslave and pillage, or in any way at all to wrong me and mine, is far more disgraceful and evil to the doer of the wrong than to me who am the sufferer. These truths, which have been already set forth as I state them in the previous discussion, would seem now to have been fixed and riveted by us, if I may use an expression which is certainly bold, in words which are like bonds of iron and adamant; and unless you or some other still more enterprising hero shall break them, there is no possibility of denying what I say. For my position has always been, that I myself am ignorant how these things are, but that I have never met any one who could say otherwise, any more than you can, and not appear ridiculous. This is my position still, and if what I am saying is true, and injustice is the greatest of evils to the doer of injustice, and yet there is if possible a greater than this greatest of evils (compare Republic), in an unjust man not suffering retribution, what is that defence of which the want will make a man truly ridiculous? Must not the defence be one which will avert the greatest of human evils? And will not the worst of all defences be that with which a man is unable to defend himself or his family or his friends?–and next will come that which is unable to avert the next greatest evil; thirdly that which is unable to avert the third greatest evil; and so of other evils. As is the greatness of evil so is the honour of being able to avert them in their several degrees, and the disgrace of not being able to avert them. Am I not right Callicles?

CALLICLES: Yes, quite right.

SOCRATES: Seeing then that there are these two evils, the doing injustice and the suffering injustice–and we affirm that to do injustice is a greater, and to suffer injustice a lesser evil–by what devices can a man succeed in obtaining the two advantages, the one of not doing and the other of not suffering injustice? must he have the power, or only the will to obtain them? I mean to ask whether a man will escape injustice if he has only the will to escape, or must he have provided himself with the power?

CALLICLES: He must have provided himself with the power; that is clear.

SOCRATES: And what do you say of doing injustice? Is the will only sufficient, and will that prevent him from doing injustice, or must he have provided himself with power and art; and if he have not studied and practised, will he be unjust still? Surely you might say, Callicles, whether you think that Polus and I were right in admitting the conclusion that no one does wrong voluntarily, but that all do wrong against their will?

CALLICLES: Granted, Socrates, if you will only have done.

SOCRATES: Then, as would appear, power and art have to be provided in order that we may do no injustice?

CALLICLES: Certainly.

SOCRATES: And what art will protect us from suffering injustice, if not wholly, yet as far as possible? I want to know whether you agree with me; for I think that such an art is the art of one who is either a ruler or even tyrant himself, or the equal and companion of the ruling power.

CALLICLES: Well said, Socrates; and please to observe how ready I am to praise you when you talk sense.

SOCRATES: Think and tell me whether you would approve of another view of mine: To me every man appears to be most the friend of him who is most like to him–like to like, as ancient sages say: Would you not agree to this?

CALLICLES: I should.

SOCRATES: But when the tyrant is rude and uneducated, he may be expected to fear any one who is his superior in virtue, and will never be able to be perfectly friendly with him.

CALLICLES: That is true.

SOCRATES: Neither will he be the friend of any one who is greatly his inferior, for the tyrant will despise him, and will never seriously regard him as a friend.

CALLICLES: That again is true.

SOCRATES: Then the only friend worth mentioning, whom the tyrant can have, will be one who is of the same character, and has the same likes and dislikes, and is at the same time willing to be subject and subservient to him; he is the man who will have power in the state, and no one will injure him with impunity:–is not that so?

CALLICLES: Yes.

SOCRATES: And if a young man begins to ask how he may become great and formidable, this would seem to be the way–he will accustom himself, from his youth upward, to feel sorrow and joy on the same occasions as his master, and will contrive to be as like him as possible?

CALLICLES: Yes.

SOCRATES: And in this way he will have accomplished, as you and your friends would say, the end of becoming a great man and not suffering injury?

CALLICLES: Very true.

SOCRATES: But will he also escape from doing injury? Must not the very opposite be true,–if he is to be like the tyrant in his injustice, and to have influence with him? Will he not rather contrive to do as much wrong as possible, and not be punished?

CALLICLES: True.

SOCRATES: And by the imitation of his master and by the power which he thus acquires will not his soul become bad and corrupted, and will not this be the greatest evil to him?

CALLICLES: You always contrive somehow or other, Socrates, to invert everything: do you not know that he who imitates the tyrant will, if he has a mind, kill him who does not imitate him and take away his goods?

SOCRATES: Excellent Callicles, I am not deaf, and I have heard that a great many times from you and from Polus and from nearly every man in the city, but I wish that you would hear me too. I dare say that he will kill him if he has a mind–the bad man will kill the good and true.

CALLICLES: And is not that just the provoking thing?

SOCRATES: Nay, not to a man of sense, as the argument shows: do you think that all our cares should be directed to prolonging life to the uttermost, and to the study of those arts which secure us from danger always; like that art of rhetoric which saves men in courts of law, and which you advise me to cultivate?

CALLICLES: Yes, truly, and very good advice too.

SOCRATES: Well, my friend, but what do you think of swimming; is that an art of any great pretensions?

CALLICLES: No, indeed.

SOCRATES: And yet surely swimming saves a man from death, and there are occasions on which he must know how to swim. And if you despise the swimmers, I will tell you of another and greater art, the art of the pilot, who not only saves the souls of men, but also their bodies and properties from the extremity of danger, just like rhetoric. Yet his art is modest and unpresuming: it has no airs or pretences of doing anything extraordinary, and, in return for the same salvation which is given by the pleader, demands only two obols, if he brings us from Aegina to Athens, or for the longer voyage from Pontus or Egypt, at the utmost two drachmae, when he has saved, as I was just now saying, the passenger and his wife and children and goods, and safely disembarked them at the Piraeus,–this is the payment which he asks in return for so great a boon; and he who is the master of the art, and has done all this, gets out and walks about on the sea-shore by his ship in an unassuming way. For he is able to reflect and is aware that he cannot tell which of his fellow-passengers he has benefited, and which of them he has injured in not allowing them to be drowned. He knows that they are just the same when he has disembarked them as when they embarked, and not a whit better either in their bodies or in their souls; and he considers that if a man who is afflicted by great and incurable bodily diseases is only to be pitied for having escaped, and is in no way benefited by him in having been saved from drowning, much less he who has great and incurable diseases, not of the body, but of the soul, which is the more valuable part of him; neither is life worth having nor of any profit to the bad man, whether he be delivered from the sea, or the law-courts, or any other devourer;–and so he reflects that such a one had better not live, for he cannot live well. (Compare Republic.)

And this is the reason why the pilot, although he is our saviour, is not usually conceited, any more than the engineer, who is not at all behind either the general, or the pilot, or any one else, in his saving power, for he sometimes saves whole cities. Is there any comparison between him and the pleader? And if he were to talk, Callicles, in your grandiose style, he would bury you under a mountain of words, declaring and insisting that we ought all of us to be engine-makers, and that no other profession is worth thinking about; he would have plenty to say. Nevertheless you despise him and his art, and sneeringly call him an engine-maker, and you will not allow your daughters to marry his son, or marry your son to his daughters. And yet, on your principle, what justice or reason is there in your refusal? What right have you to despise the engine-maker, and the others whom I was just now mentioning? I know that you will say, "I am better, and better born." But if the better is not what I say, and virtue consists only in a man saving himself and his, whatever may be his character, then your censure of the engine-maker, and of the physician, and of the other arts of salvation, is ridiculous. O my friend! I want you to see that the noble and the good may possibly be something different from saving and being saved:–May not he who is truly a man cease to care about living a certain time?–he knows, as women say, that no man can escape fate, and therefore he is not fond of life; he leaves all that with God, and considers in what way he can best spend his appointed term;–whether by assimilating himself to the constitution under which he lives, as you at this moment have to consider how you may become as like as possible to the Athenian people, if you mean to be in their good graces, and to have power in the state; whereas I want you to think and see whether this is for the interest of either of us;–I would not have us risk that which is dearest on the acquisition of this power, like the Thessalian enchantresses, who, as they say, bring down the moon from heaven at the risk of their own perdition. But if you suppose that any man will show you the art of becoming great in the city, and yet not conforming yourself to the ways of the city, whether for better or worse, then I can only say that you are mistaken, Callides; for he who would deserve to be the true natural friend of the Athenian Demus, aye, or of Pyrilampes' darling who is called after them, must be by nature like them, and not an imitator only. He, then, who will make you most like them, will make you as you desire, a statesman and orator: for every man is pleased when he is spoken to in his own language and spirit, and dislikes any other. But perhaps you, sweet Callicles, may be of another mind. What do you say?

CALLICLES: Somehow or other your words, Socrates, always appear to me to be good words; and yet, like the rest of the world, I am not quite convinced by them. (Compare Symp.: 1 Alcib.)

SOCRATES: The reason is, Callicles, that the love of Demus which abides in your soul is an adversary to me; but I dare say that if we recur to these same matters, and consider them more thoroughly, you may be convinced for all that. Please, then, to remember that there are two processes of training all things, including body and soul; in the one, as we said, we treat them with a view to pleasure, and in the other with a view to the highest good, and then we do not indulge but resist them: was not that the distinction which we drew?

CALLICLES: Very true.

SOCRATES: And the one which had pleasure in view was just a vulgar flattery:–was not that another of our conclusions?

CALLICLES: Be it so, if you will have it.

SOCRATES: And the other had in view the greatest improvement of that which was ministered to, whether body or soul?

CALLICLES: Quite true.

SOCRATES: And must we not have the same end in view in the treatment of our city and citizens? Must we not try and make them as good as possible? For we have already discovered that there is no use in imparting to them any other good, unless the mind of those who are to have the good, whether money, or office, or any other sort of power, be gentle and good. Shall we say that?

CALLICLES: Yes, certainly, if you like.

SOCRATES: Well, then, if you and I, Callicles, were intending to set about some public business, and were advising one another to undertake buildings, such as walls, docks or temples of the largest size, ought we not to examine ourselves, first, as to whether we know or do not know the art of building, and who taught us?–would not that be necessary, Callicles?

CALLICLES: True.

SOCRATES: In the second place, we should have to consider whether we had ever constructed any private house, either of our own or for our friends, and whether this building of ours was a success or not; and if upon consideration we found that we had had good and eminent masters, and had been successful in constructing many fine buildings, not only with their assistance, but without them, by our own unaided skill–in that case prudence would not dissuade us from proceeding to the construction of public works. But if we had no master to show, and only a number of worthless buildings or none at all, then, surely, it would be ridiculous in us to attempt public works, or to advise one another to undertake them. Is not this true?

CALLICLES: Certainly.

SOCRATES: And does not the same hold in all other cases? If you and I were physicians, and were advising one another that we were competent to practise as state-physicians, should I not ask about you, and would you not ask about me, Well, but how about Socrates himself, has he good health? and was any one else ever known to be cured by him, whether slave or freeman? And I should make the same enquiries about you. And if we arrived at the conclusion that no one, whether citizen or stranger, man or woman, had ever been any the better for the medical skill of either of us, then, by Heaven, Callicles, what an absurdity to think that we or any human being should be so silly as to set up as state-physicians and advise others like ourselves to do the same, without having first practised in private, whether successfully or not, and acquired experience of the art! Is not this, as they say, to begin with the big jar when you are learning the potter's art; which is a foolish thing?

CALLICLES: True.

SOCRATES: And now, my friend, as you are already beginning to be a public character, and are admonishing and reproaching me for not being one, suppose that we ask a few questions of one another. Tell me, then, Callicles, how about making any of the citizens better? Was there ever a man who was once vicious, or unjust, or intemperate, or foolish, and became by the help of Callicles good and noble? Was there ever such a man, whether citizen or stranger, slave or freeman? Tell me, Callicles, if a person were to ask these questions of you, what would you answer? Whom would you say that you had improved by your conversation? There may have been good deeds of this sort which were done by you as a private person, before you came forward in public. Why will you not answer?

CALLICLES: You are contentious, Socrates.

SOCRATES: Nay, I ask you, not from a love of contention, but because I really want to know in what way you think that affairs should be administered among us–whether, when you come to the administration of them, you have any other aim but the improvement of the citizens? Have we not already admitted many times over that such is the duty of a public man? Nay, we have surely said so; for if you will not answer for yourself I must answer for you. But if this is what the good man ought to effect for the benefit of his own state, allow me to recall to you the names of those whom you were just now mentioning, Pericles, and Cimon, and Miltiades, and Themistocles, and ask whether you still think that they were good citizens.

CALLICLES: I do.

SOCRATES: But if they were good, then clearly each of them must have made the citizens better instead of worse?

CALLICLES: Yes.

SOCRATES: And, therefore, when Pericles first began to speak in the assembly, the Athenians were not so good as when he spoke last?

CALLICLES: Very likely.

SOCRATES: Nay, my friend, "likely" is not the word; for if he was a good citizen, the inference is certain.

CALLICLES: And what difference does that make?

SOCRATES: None; only I should like further to know whether the Athenians are supposed to have been made better by Pericles, or, on the contrary, to have been corrupted by him; for I hear that he was the first who gave the people pay, and made them idle and cowardly, and encouraged them in the love of talk and money.

CALLICLES: You heard that, Socrates, from the laconising set who bruise their ears.

SOCRATES: But what I am going to tell you now is not mere hearsay, but well known both to you and me: that at first, Pericles was glorious and his character unimpeached by any verdict of the Athenians–this was during the time when they were not so good–yet afterwards, when they had been made good and gentle by him, at the very end of his life they convicted him of theft, and almost put him to death, clearly under the notion that he was a malefactor.

CALLICLES: Well, but how does that prove Pericles' badness?

SOCRATES: Why, surely you would say that he was a bad manager of asses or horses or oxen, who had received them originally neither kicking nor butting nor biting him, and implanted in them all these savage tricks? Would he not be a bad manager of any animals who received them gentle, and made them fiercer than they were when he received them? What do you say?

CALLICLES: I will do you the favour of saying "yes."

SOCRATES: And will you also do me the favour of saying whether man is an animal?

CALLICLES: Certainly he is.

SOCRATES: And was not Pericles a shepherd of men?

CALLICLES: Yes.

SOCRATES: And if he was a good political shepherd, ought not the animals who were his subjects, as we were just now acknowledging, to have become more just, and not more unjust?

CALLICLES: Quite true.

SOCRATES: And are not just men gentle, as Homer says?–or are you of another mind?

CALLICLES: I agree.

SOCRATES: And yet he really did make them more savage than he received them, and their savageness was shown towards himself; which he must have been very far from desiring.

CALLICLES: Do you want me to agree with you?

SOCRATES: Yes, if I seem to you to speak the truth.

CALLICLES: Granted then.

SOCRATES: And if they were more savage, must they not have been more unjust and inferior?

CALLICLES: Granted again.

SOCRATES: Then upon this view, Pericles was not a good statesman?

CALLICLES: That is, upon your view.

SOCRATES: Nay, the view is yours, after what you have admitted. Take the case of Cimon again. Did not the very persons whom he was serving ostracize him, in order that they might not hear his voice for ten years? and they did just the same to Themistocles, adding the penalty of exile; and they voted that Miltiades, the hero of Marathon, should be thrown into the pit of death, and he was only saved by the Prytanis. And yet, if they had been really good men, as you say, these things would never have happened to them. For the good charioteers are not those who at first keep their place, and then, when they have broken-in their horses, and themselves become better charioteers, are thrown out–that is not the way either in charioteering or in any profession.–What do you think?

CALLICLES: I should think not.

SOCRATES: Well, but if so, the truth is as I have said already, that in the Athenian State no one has ever shown himself to be a good statesman–you admitted that this was true of our present statesmen, but not true of former ones, and you preferred them to the others; yet they have turned out to be no better than our present ones; and therefore, if they were rhetoricians, they did not use the true art of rhetoric or of flattery, or they would not have fallen out of favour.

CALLICLES: But surely, Socrates, no living man ever came near any one of them in his performances.

SOCRATES: O, my dear friend, I say nothing against them regarded as the serving-men of the State; and I do think that they were certainly more serviceable than those who are living now, and better able to gratify the wishes of the State; but as to transforming those desires and not allowing them to have their way, and using the powers which they had, whether of persuasion or of force, in the improvement of their fellow citizens, which is the prime object of the truly good citizen, I do not see that in these respects they were a whit superior to our present statesmen, although I do admit that they were more clever at providing ships and walls and docks, and all that. You and I have a ridiculous way, for during the whole time that we are arguing, we are always going round and round to the same point, and constantly misunderstanding one another. If I am not mistaken, you have admitted and acknowledged more than once, that there are two kinds of operations which have to do with the body, and two which have to do with the soul: one of the two is ministerial, and if our bodies are hungry provides food for them, and if they are thirsty gives them drink, or if they are cold supplies them with garments, blankets, shoes, and all that they crave. I use the same images as before intentionally, in order that you may understand me the better. The purveyor of the articles may provide them either wholesale or retail, or he may be the maker of any of them,–the baker, or the cook, or the weaver, or the shoemaker, or the currier; and in so doing, being such as he is, he is naturally supposed by himself and every one to minister to the body. For none of them know that there is another art–an art of gymnastic and medicine which is the true minister of the body, and ought to be the mistress of all the rest, and to use their results according to the knowledge which she has and they have not, of the real good or bad effects of meats and drinks on the body. All other arts which have to do with the body are servile and menial and illiberal; and gymnastic and medicine are, as they ought to be, their mistresses. Now, when I say that all this is equally true of the soul, you seem at first to know and understand and assent to my words, and then a little while afterwards you come repeating, Has not the State had good and noble citizens? and when I ask you who they are, you reply, seemingly quite in earnest, as if I had asked, Who are or have been good trainers?–and you had replied, Thearion, the baker, Mithoecus, who wrote the Sicilian cookery-book, Sarambus, the vintner: these are ministers of the body, first-rate in their art; for the first makes admirable loaves, the second excellent dishes, and the third capital wine;–to me these appear to be the exact parallel of the statesmen whom you mention. Now you would not be altogether pleased if I said to you, My friend, you know nothing of gymnastics; those of whom you are speaking to me are only the ministers and purveyors of luxury, who have no good or noble notions of their art, and may very likely be filling and fattening men's bodies and gaining their approval, although the result is that they lose their original flesh in the long run, and become thinner than they were before; and yet they, in their simplicity, will not attribute their diseases and loss of flesh to their entertainers; but when in after years the unhealthy surfeit brings the attendant penalty of disease, he who happens to be near them at the time, and offers them advice, is accused and blamed by them, and if they could they would do him some harm; while they proceed to eulogize the men who have been the real authors of the mischief. And that, Callicles, is just what you are now doing. You praise the men who feasted the citizens and satisfied their desires, and people say that they have made the city great, not seeing that the swollen and ulcerated condition of the State is to be attributed to these elder statesmen; for they have filled the city full of harbours and docks and walls and revenues and all that, and have left no room for justice and temperance. And when the crisis of the disorder comes, the people will blame the advisers of the hour, and applaud Themistocles and Cimon and Pericles, who are the real authors of their calamities; and if you are not careful they may assail you and my friend Alcibiades, when they are losing not only their new acquisitions, but also their original possessions; not that you are the authors of these misfortunes of theirs, although you may perhaps be accessories to them.

A great piece of work is always being made, as I see and am told, now as of old; about our statesmen. When the State treats any of them as malefactors, I observe that there is a great uproar and indignation at the supposed wrong which is done to them; "after all their many services to the State, that they should unjustly perish,"–so the tale runs. But the cry is all a lie; for no statesman ever could be unjustly put to death by the city of which he is the head. The case of the professed statesman is, I believe, very much like that of the professed sophist; for the sophists, although they are wise men, are nevertheless guilty of a strange piece of folly; professing to be teachers of virtue, they will often accuse their disciples of wronging them, and defrauding them of their pay, and showing no gratitude for their services. Yet what can be more absurd than that men who have become just and good, and whose injustice has been taken away from them, and who have had justice implanted in them by their teachers, should act unjustly by reason of the injustice which is not in them? Can anything be more irrational, my friends, than this? You, Callicles, compel me to be a mob-orator, because you will not answer.

CALLICLES: And you are the man who cannot speak unless there is some one to answer?

SOCRATES: I suppose that I can; just now, at any rate, the speeches which I am making are long enough because you refuse to answer me. But I adjure you by the god of friendship, my good sir, do tell me whether there does not appear to you to be a great inconsistency in saying that you have made a man good, and then blaming him for being bad?

CALLICLES: Yes, it appears so to me.

SOCRATES: Do you never hear our professors of education speaking in this inconsistent manner?

CALLICLES: Yes, but why talk of men who are good for nothing?

SOCRATES: I would rather say, why talk of men who profess to be rulers, and declare that they are devoted to the improvement of the city, and nevertheless upon occasion declaim against the utter vileness of the city:–do you think that there is any difference between one and the other? My good friend, the sophist and the rhetorician, as I was saying to Polus, are the same, or nearly the same; but you ignorantly fancy that rhetoric is a perfect thing, and sophistry a thing to be despised; whereas the truth is, that sophistry is as much superior to rhetoric as legislation is to the practice of law, or gymnastic to medicine. The orators and sophists, as I am inclined to think, are the only class who cannot complain of the mischief ensuing to themselves from that which they teach others, without in the same breath accusing themselves of having done no good to those whom they profess to benefit. Is not this a fact?

CALLICLES: Certainly it is.

SOCRATES: If they were right in saying that they make men better, then they are the only class who can afford to leave their remuneration to those who have been benefited by them. Whereas if a man has been benefited in any other way, if, for example, he has been taught to run by a trainer, he might possibly defraud him of his pay, if the trainer left the matter to him, and made no agreement with him that he should receive money as soon as he had given him the utmost speed; for not because of any deficiency of speed do men act unjustly, but by reason of injustice.

CALLICLES: Very true.

SOCRATES: And he who removes injustice can be in no danger of being treated unjustly: he alone can safely leave the honorarium to his pupils, if he be really able to make them good–am I not right? (Compare Protag.)

CALLICLES: Yes.

SOCRATES: Then we have found the reason why there is no dishonour in a man receiving pay who is called in to advise about building or any other art?

CALLICLES: Yes, we have found the reason.

SOCRATES: But when the point is, how a man may become best himself, and best govern his family and state, then to say that you will give no advice gratis is held to be dishonourable?

CALLICLES: True.

SOCRATES: And why? Because only such benefits call forth a desire to requite them, and there is evidence that a benefit has been conferred when the benefactor receives a return; otherwise not. Is this true?

CALLICLES: It is.

SOCRATES: Then to which service of the State do you invite me? determine for me. Am I to be the physician of the State who will strive and struggle to make the Athenians as good as possible; or am I to be the servant and flatterer of the State? Speak out, my good friend, freely and fairly as you did at first and ought to do again, and tell me your entire mind.

CALLICLES: I say then that you should be the servant of the State.

SOCRATES: The flatterer? well, sir, that is a noble invitation.

CALLICLES: The Mysian, Socrates, or what you please. For if you refuse, the consequences will be–

SOCRATES: Do not repeat the old story–that he who likes will kill me and get my money; for then I shall have to repeat the old answer, that he will be a bad man and will kill the good, and that the money will be of no use to him, but that he will wrongly use that which he wrongly took, and if wrongly, basely, and if basely, hurtfully.

CALLICLES: How confident you are, Socrates, that you will never come to harm! you seem to think that you are living in another country, and can never be brought into a court of justice, as you very likely may be brought by some miserable and mean person.

SOCRATES: Then I must indeed be a fool, Callicles, if I do not know that in the Athenian State any man may suffer anything. And if I am brought to trial and incur the dangers of which you speak, he will be a villain who brings me to trial–of that I am very sure, for no good man would accuse the innocent. Nor shall I be surprised if I am put to death. Shall I tell you why I anticipate this?

CALLICLES: By all means.

SOCRATES: I think that I am the only or almost the only Athenian living who practises the true art of politics; I am the only politician of my time. Now, seeing that when I speak my words are not uttered with any view of gaining favour, and that I look to what is best and not to what is most pleasant, having no mind to use those arts and graces which you recommend, I shall have nothing to say in the justice court. And you might argue with me, as I was arguing with Polus:–I shall be tried just as a physician would be tried in a court of little boys at the indictment of the cook. What would he reply under such circumstances, if some one were to accuse him, saying, "O my boys, many evil things has this man done to you: he is the death of you, especially of the younger ones among you, cutting and burning and starving and suffocating you, until you know not what to do; he gives you the bitterest potions, and compels you to hunger and thirst. How unlike the variety of meats and sweets on which I feasted you!" What do you suppose that the physician would be able to reply when he found himself in such a predicament? If he told the truth he could only say, "All these evil things, my boys, I did for your health," and then would there not just be a clamour among a jury like that? How they would cry out!

CALLICLES: I dare say.

SOCRATES: Would he not be utterly at a loss for a reply?

CALLICLES: He certainly would.

SOCRATES: And I too shall be treated in the same way, as I well know, if I am brought before the court. For I shall not be able to rehearse to the people the pleasures which I have procured for them, and which, although I am not disposed to envy either the procurers or enjoyers of them, are deemed by them to be benefits and advantages. And if any one says that I corrupt young men, and perplex their minds, or that I speak evil of old men, and use bitter words towards them, whether in private or public, it is useless for me to reply, as I truly might:–"All this I do for the sake of justice, and with a view to your interest, my judges, and to nothing else." And therefore there is no saying what may happen to me.

CALLICLES: And do you think, Socrates, that a man who is thus defenceless is in a good position?

SOCRATES: Yes, Callicles, if he have that defence, which as you have often acknowledged he should have–if he be his own defence, and have never said or done anything wrong, either in respect of gods or men; and this has been repeatedly acknowledged by us to be the best sort of defence. And if any one could convict me of inability to defend myself or others after this sort, I should blush for shame, whether I was convicted before many, or before a few, or by myself alone; and if I died from want of ability to do so, that would indeed grieve me. But if I died because I have no powers of flattery or rhetoric, I am very sure that you would not find me repining at death. For no man who is not an utter fool and coward is afraid of death itself, but he is afraid of doing wrong. For to go to the world below having one's soul full of injustice is the last and worst of all evils. And in proof of what I say, if you have no objection, I should like to tell you a story.

CALLICLES: Very well, proceed; and then we shall have done.

SOCRATES: Listen, then, as story-tellers say, to a very pretty tale, which I dare say that you may be disposed to regard as a fable only, but which, as I believe, is a true tale, for I mean to speak the truth. Homer tells us (Il.), how Zeus and Poseidon and Pluto divided the empire which they inherited from their father. Now in the days of Cronos there existed a law respecting the destiny of man, which has always been, and still continues to be in Heaven,–that he who has lived all his life in justice and holiness shall go, when he is dead, to the Islands of the Blessed, and dwell there in perfect happiness out of the reach of evil; but that he who has lived unjustly and impiously shall go to the house of vengeance and punishment, which is called Tartarus. And in the time of Cronos, and even quite lately in the reign of Zeus, the judgment was given on the very day on which the men were to die; the judges were alive, and the men were alive; and the consequence was that the judgments were not well given. Then Pluto and the authorities from the Islands of the Blessed came to Zeus, and said that the souls found their way to the wrong places. Zeus said: "I shall put a stop to this; the judgments are not well given, because the persons who are judged have their clothes on, for they are alive; and there are many who, having evil souls, are apparelled in fair bodies, or encased in wealth or rank, and, when the day of judgment arrives, numerous witnesses come forward and testify on their behalf that they have lived righteously. The judges are awed by them, and they themselves too have their clothes on when judging; their eyes and ears and their whole bodies are interposed as a veil before their own souls. All this is a hindrance to them; there are the clothes of the judges and the clothes of the judged.–What is to be done? I will tell you:–In the first place, I will deprive men of the foreknowledge of death, which they possess at present: this power which they have Prometheus has already received my orders to take from them: in the second place, they shall be entirely stripped before they are judged, for they shall be judged when they are dead; and the judge too shall be naked, that is to say, dead–he with his naked soul shall pierce into the other naked souls; and they shall die suddenly and be deprived of all their kindred, and leave their brave attire strewn upon the earth–conducted in this manner, the judgment will be just. I knew all about the matter before any of you, and therefore I have made my sons judges; two from Asia, Minos and Rhadamanthus, and one from Europe, Aeacus. And these, when they are dead, shall give judgment in the meadow at the parting of the ways, whence the two roads lead, one to the Islands of the Blessed, and the other to Tartarus.

Rhadamanthus shall judge those who come from Asia, and Aeacus those who come from Europe. And to Minos I shall give the primacy, and he shall hold a court of appeal, in case either of the two others are in any doubt:–then the judgment respecting the last journey of men will be as just as possible."

From this tale, Callicles, which I have heard and believe, I draw the following inferences:–Death, if I am right, is in the first place the separation from one another of two things, soul and body; nothing else. And after they are separated they retain their several natures, as in life; the body keeps the same habit, and the results of treatment or accident are distinctly visible in it: for example, he who by nature or training or both, was a tall man while he was alive, will remain as he was, after he is dead; and the fat man will remain fat; and so on; and the dead man, who in life had a fancy to have flowing hair, will have flowing hair. And if he was marked with the whip and had the prints of the scourge, or of wounds in him when he was alive, you might see the same in the dead body; and if his limbs were broken or misshapen when he was alive, the same appearance would be visible in the dead. And in a word, whatever was the habit of the body during life would be distinguishable after death, either perfectly, or in a great measure and for a certain time. And I should imagine that this is equally true of the soul, Callicles; when a man is stripped of the body, all the natural or acquired affections of the soul are laid open to view.–And when they come to the judge, as those from Asia come to Rhadamanthus, he places them near him and inspects them quite impartially, not knowing whose the soul is: perhaps he may lay hands on the soul of the great king, or of some other king or potentate, who has no soundness in him, but his soul is marked with the whip, and is full of the prints and scars of perjuries and crimes with which each action has stained him, and he is all crooked with falsehood and imposture, and has no straightness, because he has lived without truth. Him Rhadamanthus beholds, full of all deformity and disproportion, which is caused by licence and luxury and insolence and incontinence, and despatches him ignominiously to his prison, and there he undergoes the punishment which he deserves.

Now the proper office of punishment is twofold: he who is rightly punished ought either to become better and profit by it, or he ought to be made an example to his fellows, that they may see what he suffers, and fear and become better. Those who are improved when they are punished by gods and men, are those whose sins are curable; and they are improved, as in this world so also in another, by pain and suffering; for there is no other way in which they can be delivered from their evil. But they who have been guilty of the worst crimes, and are incurable by reason of their crimes, are made examples; for, as they are incurable, the time has passed at which they can receive any benefit. They get no good themselves, but others get good when they behold them enduring for ever the most terrible and painful and fearful sufferings as the penalty of their sins–there they are, hanging up as examples, in the prison-house of the world below, a spectacle and a warning to all unrighteous men who come thither. And among them, as I confidently affirm, will be found Archelaus, if Polus truly reports of him, and any other tyrant who is like him. Of these fearful examples, most, as I believe, are taken from the class of tyrants and kings and potentates and public men, for they are the authors of the greatest and most impious crimes, because they have the power. And Homer witnesses to the truth of this; for they are always kings and potentates whom he has described as suffering everlasting punishment in the world below: such were Tantalus and Sisyphus and Tityus. But no one ever described Thersites, or any private person who was a villain, as suffering everlasting punishment, or as incurable. For to commit the worst crimes, as I am inclined to think, was not in his power, and he was happier than those who had the power. No, Callicles, the very bad men come from the class of those who have power (compare Republic). And yet in that very class there may arise good men, and worthy of all admiration they are, for where there is great power to do wrong, to live and to die justly is a hard thing, and greatly to be praised, and few there are who attain to this. Such good and true men, however, there have been, and will be again, at Athens and in other states, who have fulfilled their trust righteously; and there is one who is quite famous all over Hellas, Aristeides, the son of Lysimachus. But, in general, great men are also bad, my friend.

As I was saying, Rhadamanthus, when he gets a soul of the bad kind, knows nothing about him, neither who he is, nor who his parents are; he knows only that he has got hold of a villain; and seeing this, he stamps him as curable or incurable, and sends him away to Tartarus, whither he goes and receives his proper recompense. Or, again, he looks with admiration on the soul of some just one who has lived in holiness and truth; he may have been a private man or not; and I should say, Callicles, that he is most likely to have been a philosopher who has done his own work, and not troubled himself with the doings of other men in his lifetime; him Rhadamanthus sends to the Islands of the Blessed. Aeacus does the same; and they both have sceptres, and judge; but Minos alone has a golden sceptre and is seated looking on, as Odysseus in Homer declares that he saw him:

"Holding a sceptre of gold, and giving laws to the dead."

Now I, Callicles, am persuaded of the truth of these things, and I consider how I shall present my soul whole and undefiled before the judge in that day. Renouncing the honours at which the world aims, I desire only to know the truth, and to live as well as I can, and, when I die, to die as well as I can. And, to the utmost of my power, I exhort all other men to do the same. And, in return for your exhortation of me, I exhort you also to take part in the great combat, which is the combat of life, and greater than every other earthly conflict. And I retort your reproach of me, and say, that you will not be able to help yourself when the day of trial and judgment, of which I was speaking, comes upon you; you will go before the judge, the son of Aegina, and, when he has got you in his grip and is carrying you off, you will gape and your head will swim round, just as mine would in the courts of this world, and very likely some one will shamefully box you on the ears, and put upon you any sort of insult.

Perhaps this may appear to you to be only an old wife's tale, which you will contemn. And there might be reason in your contemning such tales, if by searching we could find out anything better or truer: but now you see that you and Polus and Gorgias, who are the three wisest of the Greeks of our day, are not able to show that we ought to live any life which does not profit in another world as well as in this. And of all that has been said, nothing remains unshaken but the saying, that to do injustice is more to be avoided than to suffer injustice, and that the reality and not the appearance of virtue is to be followed above all things, as well in public as in private life; and that when any one has been wrong in anything, he is to be chastised, and that the next best thing to a man being just is that he should become just, and be chastised and punished; also that he should avoid all flattery of himself as well as of others, of the few or of the many: and rhetoric and any other art should be used by him, and all his actions should be done always, with a view to justice.

Follow me then, and I will lead you where you will be happy in life and after death, as the argument shows. And never mind if some one despises you as a fool, and insults you, if he has a mind; let him strike you, by Zeus, and do you be of good cheer, and do not mind the insulting blow, for you will never come to any harm in the practice of virtue, if you are a really good and true man. When we have practised virtue together, we will apply ourselves to politics, if that seems desirable, or we will advise about whatever else may seem good to us, for we shall be better able to judge then. In our present condition we ought not to give ourselves airs, for even on the most important subjects we are always changing our minds; so utterly stupid are we! Let us, then, take the argument as our guide, which has revealed to us that the best way of life is to practise justice and every virtue in life and death. This way let us go; and in this exhort all men to follow, not in the way to which you trust and in which you exhort me to follow you; for that way, Callicles, is nothing worth.